The Promise and the Plow

THE PROMISE AND THE PLOW

Mary E. Judson

Horizon House Publishers
Camp Hill, Pennsylvania

Horizon House Publishers
3825 Hartzdale Drive
Camp Hill, PA 17011

ISBN: 0-88965-088-8

© 1990 by Horizon House Publishers
All rights reserved
Printed in the United States of America

90 91 92 93 94 5 4 3 2 1

Cover illustration by
Step One Design, Brenda Wintermyer

Unless otherwise indicated, Scripture taken from the
HOLY BIBLE: NEW INTERNATIONAL VERSION.
Copyright © 1973, 1978, 1984 by the International
Bible Society. Used by permission of
Zondervan Bible Publishers

Dedication

To my husband, Reuben
whose counsel and support
made this book possible.

Acknowledgements

To my sister, Margaret McMurray, whose stedfast commitment and support of our ministry, both financial and spiritual, was an encouragement to us.

To the many friends who urged me to write this book.

To Mrs. Marilynne Foster of Christian Publications, for her guidance and understanding.

This almost-true story focuses on commitment and faithfulness—the commitment of a determined young woman to the will of God and the faithfulness of a loving heavenly Father to the one who obeyed Him.

The names of geographical places in the Philippines are factual, but names of persons have been changed.

*"No man who puts his hand to the plow
and looks back is fit for service
in the kingdom of God."
(Luke 9:62)*

FOREWORD

You are in for a treat.

The Promise and the Plow vividly portrays the emotions, trials and triumphs of a brave young woman captured and commissioned by the Master who said, "Go . . . and lo, I am with you always. . . ."

Dr. Mary Judson is uniquely qualified to write of the price and privilege of obedience to Jesus Christ. As a single missionary in the Philippines, Mary knew the thrills and chills of bearing the gospel to tribal people who had never heard.

Using fictional characters to live out actual experiences, the author cleverly weaves together a story line which reveals the rewards of those are willing to put their hand to the plow and prove the faithfulness of God.

God brought Mary and her husband, Reuben, into my life more than forty years ago. Their maturity and godly example were invaluable to this high-spirited young missionary. My wife and I served 24 years as co-laborers with the Judsons in Manila and leaned on them for counsel and prayer support.

This one-evening novel challenges all who follow Christ to tighten their grip on the plow and never turn back.

Charles A. Hufstetler
U.S. Director
SEND International

1

Kerry glanced around, her heart pounding. Other passengers on the S.S. Madison were strolling the decks or tossing colorful balls of confetti to the well-wishers on the pier below. Her own family and friends had said their goodbyes when she boarded the train (could it have been only 10 days ago?) in Albany, New York.

Here in San Francisco, she was among strangers. In all the seething mass before her, the only face she recognized was that of the mission executive farewelling a small party of missionaries, including herself, enroute to the Far East.

It was six years since she had first felt the call of God for missionary service. In all that time she had never doubted His leading. But right now, stark apprehension gripped her. All that had gone before—her training, travels, and visiting the churches—had brought her to this day of reckoning. She was actually leaving all she knew and loved to go half-way around the world to serve God in the Philippines! And she was scared, very vulnerable and terribly alone.

Suddenly the ship's whistle gave a piercing blast. Kerry jumped! *What on earth am I doing going so far away from home? Oh, if I could only get off this ship!*

Just then Kerry noticed a small girl standing a few feet in front of her. The child's gaze was fastened on the pier and she was waving. She had been waving so long that her arm was tired. "I can't see him, Mommy," Kerry heard her say, "but I know he's there."

In that instant, the Lord Jesus spoke to Kerry, "You can't see Me, My child, but I'm right here!"

That was a promise she would count on many times in the years to come.

2

Kerry Kathleen McCormick was the fifth child in a family of six. As in many large middle-class families, money was often scarce, but there was no lack of love. With wholesome food to eat and clothes to wear the McCormick children never thought of themselves as deprived. Their home rang with their laughter and creaked and groaned with their play.

Then overnight everything changed. Laura McCormick, mother of this healthy, happy tribe, was rushed to a nearby hospital. The diagnosis—a blood clot to the brain. Within hours, Laura breathed her last.

The shock to the family was enormous. Kerry herself didn't really comprehend what had happened. Why was the house strangely hushed except for the muffled sounds of weeping? Why were the faces pale and downcast? Why wasn't her mother there to put her arms around her and reassure her with her smile? But her mother had gone to heaven, they told her. Looking up at the distant clouds she wondered with a childish mind how big a ladder she would need to climb up there and bring her back.

Her mother's death left a gnawing pain in six-year-old Kerry's heart. Baby Tracy cried incessantly for "Mama" and refused to be comforted. Kerry did her best to hold back her own tears, but the pain wouldn't go away. Every time she saw her playmate's mother buttoning up her coat or fastening her boots, a huge lump would swell in Kerry's throat.

Her father, George McCormick, though crushed with grief, determined to keep his motherless brood together. This was no easy task, but then George was no ordinary man. He loved his children dearly and every child knew he would not spare the rod if they stepped out of line. Kerry adored this tall, handsome father of hers and she tried hard to please him. But she was a high-spirited child and found it downright next to impossible to keep out of mischief! It was a rare day when she was not warned by one of her siblings, "You just wait till Daddy gets home. You're gonna get it!" Kerry, with a bravado she was far from feeling, would shrug her shoulders, toss her dark curls and skip off. Never would she give them the satisfaction of seeing that their warning scared her!

The neighbor ladies were concerned for the McCormick children and most of all for Kerry. "Just look at that child," they would say, "tearing around and hollering like an Indian!" Then with a foreboding shake of the head, "Makes one wonder what will ever become of her!"

That was a good question. Kerry wondered too. During her high school days, she dabbled in fine arts until forced to take mechanical drawing. She hated the subject—she was the only girl enrolled in the class. At one point, her father tried to interest her in office work. That bored her to death. As for teaching, that was certainly out. She did like to write, but even better than writing stories would be acting them out! Kerry always loved drama. As a small child she would climb on a chair and perform in front of the big mirror on the wall. Fascinated by her own image, she would run through a gamut of emotions: joy, grief, anger, fear, indignation. Her twin brothers would howl with delight.

The first time she had a part in a Sunday School program, Kerry refused to leave the platform even when her teacher tugged at her sleeve. This delighted the audience. Their laughter pleased and excited her. Clearly the stage had had an appeal for her then. Now, at seventeen, Kerry could think of nothing more thrilling than a stage career.

3

Supper at the McCormick household was usually a happy event, the only meal of the day when the entire family was together. It was an iron-clad rule that every member be present and on time. At the stroke of six, George McCormick would take his place at the head of the table and check to make sure no one was missing. There was Sue, the eldest, very much like her mother. Beth, quiet and patient, making no effort to join in the lively chatter. Next, the good-looking twins, Tim and Tom. Then Kerry, Irish-blue eyes dancing, and last but not least, dainty Tracy. Satisfied, George would begin serving.

"How did football practice go today?" father asked the twins.

Tim answered with a shrug, "No practice today. We're not playing this weekend."

"I see. Who will be playing?"

"Bennett High and Parkside." Tim winked at his father and glanced furtively at Kerry. "Sure won't be much competition in that game!"

"You'd better believe it!" echoed Tom. "Poor old Bennett is sure to get creamed!"

All of this was for Kerry's benefit who was in her junior year at Bennett High. She was fiercely loyal to her school and at the same time painfully embarrassed because of their poor showing on the football field.

"Don't let them get to you, daughter. I'm rooting for Bennett High too!" Dad assured her.

"Dad, you've got to be kidding," spouted Tim, "they don't have a prayer!"

Kerry's eyes flashed. "Maybe we will get creamed," she said icily, "and maybe, just maybe, you two smart-alecks are in for a big surprise!" Casting a pleading look at her father, she stalked out of the room.

"Hey, take it easy fellas. You've been

riding her pretty hard. Why not pick on somebody else for change? You've got three other sisters, you know."

"Yeah, we know, but they don't get mad. Kerry's a lot more fun!"

4

The air was crisp with a November chill. Kerry and Tracy grabbed their jackets and started out for the weekly visit at Vic's, the corner drug store and ice cream parlor. Vic's was popular with the high school crowd.

As the girls entered the store, they could feel admiring glances. Tracy, now fifteen, was the only blond in the McCormick family. Her brown eyes and dark lashes and brows were in vivid contrast to the gold of her hair. She was a small girl and her daintiness and coloring lent an air of fragility. Kerry, on the other hand, was the spitting image of her father. The same dark curly hair, the same intensely blue eyes, thickly fringed, the same mouth and firm chin. Unlike Tracy, she was tall for her age, with a lithe body, bursting with vigor. "A chip off the old block," relatives said. "The girl and her father are as alike as two peas in a pod!"

Kerry and Tracy gave their orders—the usual pineapple-cherry sundaes smothered with whipped cream. Within minutes the sundaes were on the counter. At that precise moment the curtain went up on Act One of Kerry's fondest dream.

"Kerry! Look! Over by the cash register. That's him, Jack Allen, the dream boat I've been telling you about!"

Kerry's glance took in the brown curly hair, the all-american profile, athletic build and broad shoulders. Nodding approval she whispered back, "You're right. He **is** gorgeous. Every bit as nice as you said!"

Just then a male voice interrupted their conversation. "You two going to the game tomorrow to watch Bennett get beat?"

A loud guffaw followed, cut short by Kerry's response. "You guys wanna bet?" Her fair skin flushed crimson. Cupping her cheeks in her hands, she muttered, "What am I saying? I don't make bets!"

"Aw, what's a bet between friends?" Fred Burke asked. "What'll it be, Kerry? One of Vic's super sundaes?"

"Surely you're not going through with this," hissed Tracy, disapproval written all over her face. To add to the confusion, they heard Jack say, "Count me in on that!"

Kerry glanced at Tracy. With a defiant shrug of her shoulders, she answered, "Okay. You're on."

They were no sooner out of the store when Tracy began: "You know what your trouble is, Kerry? You speak before you think!"

Kerry turned angrily, "Do you think I wanted to make that bet? It's their fault. They made me mad."

"So, what else is new?" Tracy waggled a slim finger at her sister. "Mark my words, that temper of yours will get you into real trouble one of these days."

5

The day of the big game came. Kerry found a good seat, waved to friends, and riveted her eyes on the field below. The school band was there, all decked out in green and gold. The players dashed out of the bunkers. The band struck up the school song. The cheerleaders went into frenzied action. Everyone, including Kerry, was on their feet, screaming and clapping and cheering.

It proved to be a good game. For once Bennett played exceptionally well. In fact, they won the game. Kerry was thrilled. It was such a delicious feeling after months of frustration. Back at Vic's she was relieved to find that neither Fred nor Jack were there. To her dismay, however, within minutes Jack strode through the door and came directly to her table. Without waiting for an invitation, he sat down. "Time I took care of that bet! I do owe you this, you know."

Kerry giggled. "Okay, Jack, pay your honest debt!" Jack smiled, and again Kerry noted his handsome good looks. *I like him*, she decided.

Kerry learned that Jack had graduated from Tech High and was now a freshman at college. His parents were English right from old sod. He had one sister a few years older than he. Jack knew Kerry's brothers and spoke admiringly of their skill on the football field. But Jack knew someone else too. He knew Jesus Christ as his Lord and Savior. "I'll be playing the violin at our Christmas program. Would you like to come along?" he invited.

Kerry was dumbfounded. Jack had no way of knowing that the McCormicks never attended church, that any prospect of such a thing disappeared the day God took her mother away. Yes, they had all attended faithfully before that. Her parents had taken them all to Sunday School and they stayed for the worship service as well. Her mother had even taught her the little prayer,

> Now I lay me down to sleep,
> I pray the Lord my soul to keep.
> If I should die before I wake,
> I pray the Lord my soul to take.

Kerry recalled too how the family used to bow their heads and give thanks to God for their food. But that was many years ago. God had no part in their life now, and what's more, they liked it that way. She would not accept Jack's invitation.

Fastening her eyes on him, eyes that had suddenly grown cold, she asked, "Just why are you interested in my going to church?"

Jack hesitated briefly, then responded. "We have a great group of young people there. I think you would like them."

"What church do you go to?" Kerry wondered aloud. She was hoping he would say Catholic or Jewish so she could refuse on the grounds that her family was Protestant. But Jack didn't say either one. Instead she was hearing the name of the very church her family used to attend while her mother was alive! Memories of her mother swept over her. Yes, her mother would want her to go.

"Okay, I'll go!" She finally responded.

Kerry felt that every eye was on her as the kids gathered for their meeting. Nervous and uncomfortable, she sat staring straight ahead hoping she wasn't showing how foreign everything was to her. The service that followed was even worse, especially the sermon. The subject was judgment and hell.

Kerry didn't believe in hell. Her father had taught his children that the only hell was right here on earth, and if her father—the dearest, wisest man on earth—said there was no hell, then that was that. As far as Kerry was concerned, the preacher was getting all steamed up over something that didn't even exist.

On the short walk home Kerry was silent. Jack finally broke in. "Well, what did you think of the sermon?"

The question brought Kerry up short. Looking at Jack directly she said, "Jack, you're a college student. Do you mean to tell me you believe in hell?"

"Yes, I do. The Bible teaches there is a

place of judgment for unrepentant people and I believe the Bible!"

His admission startled Kerry. She had never met a young person who admitted faith in the teachings of the Bible.

It was a thoughtful Kerry who turned the doorknob. Jack headed for home. "She's a little heathen! A mighty pretty heathen," he muttered, jamming his hands into his coat pockets and squaring his broad shoulders. "But I'm out to change that."

6

The following Sunday morning, before Kerry was even out of bed, the doorbell rang. It was Edith, Jack's sister, inviting her to join them for Sunday School and the morning worship service.

"But, I'm not ready!" protested Kerry.

"Oh, I'll wait," responded Edith cheerfully. "If you hurry we can make it." With that, she plopped into a nearby chair.

What gall, what absolute gall! Kerry thought as she headed back upstairs. *I suppose Jack sent her.* Then in spite of her irritation, she chuckled, "The family will never believe this. Me, in church, two Sundays in a row!"

As the young people parted at noon, Edith said, "Youth meeting is at 6:30. We'd love to have you go with us!" And so it went for four Sundays: Sunday School, morning service, youth meeting, evening service.

"You're there all day. Why not take your bed and stay all night?" complained Kerry's father.

As Kerry continued to sit under the preaching of the gospel strange things began to happen. The Spirit of God was convincing her. She had always thought of herself as a "good" girl who had been raised in a morally strict home. But she was learning, at least according to the pastor, that being morally good was not good enough. She was a sinner in need of a Savior and that Savior was Jesus Christ. The Holy Spirit was preparing her for the pastor's searching question, "Young lady, don't you think it is time you gave your heart to Jesus?"

The struggle was brief. Kerry lifted tear-filled eyes and said softly, "I know it's time." Down at the altar, the pastor explained God's way of salvation. Kerry, who had not prayed since that simple prayer at her mother's knee, asked for forgiveness and cleansing and by faith received the gift of eternal life. When she rose from her knees, Kerry knew that God had heard her prayer. She was a new creature in Christ Jesus!

Walking home that night, Kerry quietly savored her new-found peace and joy. Tracy brought her back to earth: "I guess you know this settles your acting career. No more Hollywood for you."

Right then a wonderful thing happened—Kerry wanted more than anything else to please God! "Whatever the Lord wants, Tracy, that's what I want to do!"

Tracy stopped. This wasn't the Kerry she knew!

Indeed it wasn't.

7

During the next six months, Kerry's love for her Savior grew. She was learning many new things. Nevertheless, she was surprised when God spoke to her in an almost audible voice.

The church had scheduled a week of special meetings. There were to be two speakers, an evangelist and a missionary. As far as Kerry could remember, she had never even seen a missionary, much less heard one. Somewhere along the line she had been told that missionaries were queer misfits who left their homeland to go all over the world and live with the heathen!

From her vantage point on the platform with the rest of the choir, Kerry watched the people file into the auditorium. She wondered if she would be able to spot the missionary. Just what she was looking for she wasn't sure.

The missionary didn't look anything like Kerry had imagined. She was young, trim and smartly dressed, and from the moment Kerry laid eyes on her, she felt an unusual attraction.

The missionary's text was Romans 10, verses 13 and 14: "How, then, can they call on the one they have not believed in? And how can they believe in the one of whom they have not heard? And how can they hear without someone preaching to them?"

"How shall they hear?" the missionary asked. "There are still those in my tribe who have never once heard the Name of Jesus Christ!"

Kerry was aghast! Had she heard correctly? After 1900 years were there still people who had never heard of Jesus? Her eyes swept over the crowd seated before her. *Why are all these people sitting here then? Why haven't some of them gone to tell the heathen?*

A voice responded. "My child I want *you* to go!"

Kerry sat rigid, petrified. Could it be happening? Her father had warned her about this. A voice saying "Go", a heavy hand weighing her down. It came again, "I want *you* to go and you must tell your father tonight!"

Through her tears Kerry responded, *Lord, if you are asking me to go for You, I'll go.* The pressure lifted. The service went on, but Kerry was unaware of anything else that was said. Later, at the altar, she knelt in prayer and affirmed her submission to the will of God.

"Dry those tears, Kerry," said the pastor. "Serving Jesus Christ is the greatest privilege on earth!"

"I suppose so," she responded weakly, "but I don't know where to begin."

"Well, before you buy your ticket, you'll have to get some training. Bible school is the first step."

Kerry shook her head, "No pastor, the first thing is to tell my father—tonight!"

As she approached the house, Kerry sent up a desperate cry. Her dad was at the dining room table, along with the twins and two of their friends. "Hello, Babe," he said cheerily, using the pet name he reserved for his daughters.

She stood there a moment, scarcely breathing. "Something on your mind?" he asked.

Her voice quivered as she blurted out, "Dad, I want to go to Bible School this fall to prepare for missionary service."

George slowly lowered his cards, smiled a forced smile, and said lightly, "I think we can manage that."

Kerry, sensing that she was dismissed, left the room. *Did he understand me? Does he really mean it? It seems too good to be true!*

Back in the dining room, George offered the boys an explanation: "You know Kerry. If I oppose her in this, she will be all the more determined to do it! If I seem to go along with the idea, it's my guess she will soon forget about it."

George McCormick certainly hoped he was right.

8

Not for a moment did Kerry forget. Instead, the desire grew and five months later Kerry found herself enrolled at a Bible college in New York state. Her father, in a last ditch effort to stop her, made it clear that she could not expect any financial assistance from him. "Not a penny," he warned, "that's final!" However, the church gave her a generous love offering and she enrolled as a working student. It was difficult working and trying to keep up the studies. However, there was still time for romance!

Brad Lange was attracted to Kerry from

the start. It was not only her physical beauty that drew him, but her love for Jesus Christ and her dedication to His cause. Often Kerry found Brad's dark eyes looking at her. She admired him, too, his keen, incisive mind and enthusiastic appreciation for Bible truth. In short, these two seemed to be on the same wave length. It was not long before friendship developed into an affair of the heart.

But there was one hitch—Kerry's insistence that God wanted her on some mission field. Brad had a heart for missions too, but felt he was called to ministry in North America. So the question was a nagging one: how would it all work out?

Kerry cared for Brad, but enough to marry him? She wasn't sure. Their lives were in God's hands. He could be trusted to work out His highest will.

As graduation approached, the candidates for overseas missionary service were interviewed by the Mission Board. Kerry waited anxiously for some report of the results. Two weeks passed and still nothing. Brad could wait no longer. Approaching a board member, Brad asked about Kerry's status. The man was sympathetic, but replied that it was out of order to notify anyone before the candidate. Brad's face fell. Seeing his disappointment, the man relented. "Well, Miss McCormick has been accepted for missionary work in the Philippines."

Brad turned away. There was no need for anyone to interpret the "handwriting on the wall." He must see Kerry at once. What would she think?

The opportunity came after dinner. "I spoke to Dr. Davidson today."

"Oh, Brad, what did he say?"

"They're giving you the green light!"

"You mean I've been accepted?" Kerry's face lit up and Brad's heart sank. "Yes, you're accepted, and I want to know what you're going to do about it?"

Kerry looked into his eyes, fighting for composure. When the answer finally came, it was a scripture verse, " 'No man who puts his hand to the plow and looks back is fit for service in the kingdom of God.' Do I have a choice, Brad?"

9

Kerry spent a sleepless night. She liked Brad very much, but she was under orders and her life was not her own. As the hours dragged by and she faced the impending separation, the words of another verse came to her: "If anyone would come after me, he must deny himself and take up his cross daily and follow me" (Luke 9:23).

Brad joined her the following morning in the dining room. It was evident from the dark circles under his eyes that he hadn't slept much either. But his smile was like always. He handed her an envelope. Inside was a poem.

Laid on Thy altar, O my Lord Divine,
Accept my gift this day, for Jesus sake:
I have no jewels to adorn Thy shrine,
Nor any world-famed sacrifice to make:
But here I bring within my trembling hands
This will of mine, a thing that seemeth small,
Yet Thou alone, O Lord, canst under stand
How, when I yield Thee this, I yield Thee all.

Hidden therein, Thy searching gaze can see
Struggles of passion, visions of delight,
All that I have, or fain would be,
Deep loves, fond hopes, and longing infinities;
It hath been wet with tears, and dimmed with sighs,
Clenched in my grasp 'till beauty has none;
Now from Thy footstools, where it vanquished lies,
The prayer ascendeth, "May Thy will be done."*

---

* The above poem was found among the papers of an African missionary after his death.

It was signed simply, "Forever Brad." The struggle was over. He too had yielded to the will of God.

In spite of the ache in her heart, Kerry whispered, "Thank you, Jesus, for giving us the strength to accept Your will."

10

Weeks streaked by. Before Kerry knew it, graduation day dawned. She should have been happy, but instead her heart was torn. Oh yes, she would prize that well-earned sheepskin all right. No question about that! But she had learned to love this place and the thought of leaving it brought genuine sorrow.

Her memory went back four years. Life had become increasingly difficult for her at home because of the resentment of her family over her Christian commitment. The closeness and sense of belonging was gone. She was like an alien in her father's house.

But the college had become a haven where she could read the Bible openly and pray and breathe the atmosphere of heaven where there was no sardonic, accusing voice. The Lord Jesus had become very real. Kerry had learned that she could count on His faithfulness. Now it was over. In a few hours she would leave these halls of learning to return to her family at home. That prospect was bitter-sweet.

Kerry watched the joyous reunion of parents with graduates. As she listened to their squeals of pleasure, her own loneliness increased. There would be no McCormicks present to rejoice with her. There had been no communication at all, not even a congratulations card.

A voice reverberated down the empty hallway. "Kerry, Kerry McCormick." There followed a pounding at her door. "Kerry, are you there?"

Kerry threw the door open. An underclassman stood there, a long white box in his arms. "Here you are," he said, thrusting the box at Kerry. "The florist just brought this. It's for you!"

Kerry's hands trembled as she untied the string. There, under folds of tissue, lay one dozen beautiful yellow roses. Her favorite! The card inside read, "Love, from Dad."

It was a radiant Kerry who donned cap and gown and assembled with the others in the school chapel. One male member of the class gave a low whistle and remarked, "Whew, those flowers must have been from someone very special!"

"Someone very special indeed!" Kerry responded. "Someone I love very much—my Dad!"

"Your Dad?" chorused several. "A likely story!"

The strains of *Pomp and Circumstance* were already filling the room. The graduates queued up, adjusted their caps and the processional began.

11

It was the rule of the Mission that all candidates for overseas service spend two years in North America before proceeding to their appointed country. The reason for this was twofold: to gain practical experience under supervision and to raise financial and prayer support.

Kerry was staggered when she learned the awesome amount she would have to raise. Her family thought it was hilarious. "You'll be an old grey-haired lady by the time you raise that amount," chortled Tim.

Tom picked up the refrain, "Yeah, what do you plan to do? Rob a bank?" The general consensus was that she would never make it.

"Looks like this settles it, thank God!" Kerry's father added.

But, of course, they were totally unaware of the power of believing prayer. Kerry had scarcely gotten her suitcase unpacked before the invitations to speak began to arrive. She was a forceful, appealing speaker and calls were soon coming from far and wide. Before the two years were over, the needed support was on hand.

Kerry's family was impressed, but none of them had indicated any interest in spiritual matters. Kerry's heart was heavy. Every day her anguished cry before God was, "How can I expect to win the heathen to You, when I can't even reach my own family?" To all appearances, none of them were any nearer the kingdom than they had been six years earlier.

Kerry's passage was booked on the S.S. Madison. It would sail from San Francisco on January 31. Now she was faced with the task of getting her outfit together. Number one on her list was a big sturdy trunk. As she approached the store checkout, a thought came to her mind—she should buy her sister Sue a Bible. Kerry tried to brush the impression aside. It would not go away. So, with the Bible in hand, she returned home.

"Did you get the trunk?" Sue met her at the door.

"Yes, and Sue, I bought something for you." Kerry handed her a package. When Sue finally looked up, her eyes were swimming with tears. Haltingly she told Kerry that although she had tried hard not to show it, she had been under deep conviction for several months. "I know God is speaking to me, but I am confused, Kerry. Today, after you left, I went to my room, got down on my knees and asked God to show me the way. This," she said, holding out the Bible, "is the answer to my prayer!"

That very night Sue gave her heart to Jesus Christ!

Life took on new meaning for Kerry after Sue's conversion. On a speaking tour in Pennsylvania, she received a letter from little sister, Tracy. She could hardly believe her eyes.

"You've been having great experiences, sis, but I want to tell you what happened to Beth and me last Sunday night when we gave our hearts to Jesus!"

Kerry thought she would explode! She

read on, "Ever since Sue got saved, Beth and I have talked about becoming Christians too. We had it all figured out—no crying, no hysterics. In a business-like way we would walk down to the altar during the invitation and ask the Lord to save us. But it didn't turn out that way. As soon as my knees hit the floor, I began to bawl. I looked over at Beth and she was bawling too! The preacher remarked, 'It's always a good thing when a new born baby cries!' Well, we cried all right, but the important and wonderful thing is that the Lord Jesus heard our prayer and washed our sins away! Now we know we belong to Him, and we are praying that the twins and Dad will soon open their hearts to the Savior, too!"

"Thank You, dear Jesus, thank you," was all that Kerry could say.

12

Leaving would have been easier for Kerry if the McCormicks had been more sympathetic to God's will for her life. Her father, especially, was understandably concerned and certainly opposed. To see one so young (and single) going so far away to face hardships and danger was extremely worrisome. Kerry tried to assure him that God, Who had called her, would care for her. But this only met with stony silence.

It was Kerry's last day at home. The atmosphere was charged with emotion. Efforts to spread a little cheer were futile.

Several times Kerry sought the privacy of her room. Her refuge was the darkened closet where none could hear her sobbing out her grief. Each time, the words of Frances Havergal came quietly to her mind, "I gave My Life for thee. What hast thou given for Me?" Kerry knew she owed her Savior a debt she could never repay. She dried her tears and returned to her family below.

Dinner that night was a disaster. Sue had prepared a delicious meal, but appetites were strangely missing. The family toyed with their food. When Dad abruptly pushed back his chair and left the room, the rest followed.

All too soon the time for departure arrived. It was planned that Kerry's sisters would accompany her to the train station. Kerry would say the rest of the goodbyes at home.

She turned to Tim. He folded her in a warm embrace, saying huskily, "Take care of yourself, kid. Don't take any wooden nickels."

Tom hugged her hard. "Wish I were going with you—no snow to shovel!"

Then, standing on tiptoe, Kerry kissed her

father. "Bye Dad. I'll keep in touch. I love you!" And she was out the door.

"Train for Buffalo, Detroit, Chicago, leaving in 15 minutes. Passengers proceed to gate number seven." Chicago was the first stop for Kerry. She would change trains there for San Francisco. As the call came over the loud speaker, Sue, Beth, and Tracy tooks turns embracing their sister.

"Call when you reach Frisco so we know you made it okay."

"You can count on our prayers, sis. God bless you!"

"Don't forget to write—often!"

Kerry's feet were like lead as she boarded the train. Finding a seat near a window, she scanned the crowd for a last glimpse of her sisters. There they were—bravely smiling and waving.

Please God, help me to be brave too. Kerry's vision suddenly blurred.

13

The sun was low in the sky when the S.S. Madison slid under the Golden Gate bridge and headed for open sea. It was a glorious sunset. Twenty-five-year-old Kerry joined the other new missionaries in admiring the panorama of vivid colors lighting up sea and sky. All were enroute to the Orient, all for the first time. The only man in the party was Cliff Pardington, who along with his wife and infant son was bound for Japan. Ellen Reed, a single girl about Kerry's age, was headed for Hong Kong. Ellen and Kerry would be roommates on the long trip.

The western sky was dark when Kerry remembered the letter. Sue had pressed it into her hand during those last moments at the train station. Excusing herself, she headed to her stateroom and drew the letter out of her handbag.

My precious sister:
Today there is great rejoicing in my heart that God has called one from our home to carry the wonderful gospel message to the regions beyond! God has certainly given me victory over our parting, and instead of sadness, He has put peace in my soul. I turned to Psalm 46 this morning, and read, "Be still and know that I am God, I will be exalted among the nations, I will be exalted in the earth." O how glad I am , Kerry dear, that we, your sisters, know Him! We shall meet daily at the Throne for your every need. I am sending you my love and a great big hug and kiss. When on board, as you read this, remember that there are three in Albany who love you very dearly. God bless you always.
Your sister, Sue.

It struck on a Sunday when the ship was located several hundred miles off the coast of Japan. The ocean had been churning wildly all day. The sky was dark and threatening. Those who had found their sea legs watched breathlessly as the vessel climbed mountainous walls of water and then plummeted to dizzying depths. It was obvious that this was no ordinary storm.

Since sleeping was out of the question, Kerry and her friends gathered in the lounge around the piano which fortunately was roped to the wall.

Crash! It was as if two ships collided! The ropes that held the piano snapped. Some alert friends prevented the piano from falling directly on Kerry. Simultaneously the cargo shifted, causing the ship to tilt at a twenty-degree angle. White-faced passengers rushed here and there while the captain and several of his officers tried to encourage them that the situation was under control. It was hard to accept when everything not nailed down was on the move!

Kerry made her way out to an enclosed deck where the wind, like a thousand human voices, shreiked around her. It was a comfort to remember that one day Jesus had stilled a storm on the Sea of Galilee.

The clock struck three before the storm abated. Later in the day, Kerry penned this note to her family:

Dear loved ones:

Did someone say an ocean voyage is fun? About ten p.m. last night we were hit by a typhoon. I thought any moment the old boat would sink. I am very thankful that the 'Master of the ocean and earth and sky' was on board to bring us safely through.

14

The ship's anchor clanked loudly. The noise startled Ellen from a fitful sleep. Today she would reach her destination. Instantly she was awake and out of bed, peering out of the porthole. It was still dark except for the myriad of twinkling lights encircling the harbor and hills beyond. "Hong Kong at last!" Ellen whispered as a sob caught in her throat.

Instinctively she reached out and shook Kerry. "Wake up! Get up! We're here!"

Kerry groaned and pulled the covers over her head.

"Come on, sleepy head. We're in Hong Kong! Let's go out on deck!" urged Ellen.

"At this hour? What time is it?"

"Who cares? Are you coming or do I have to go alone?" Thrusting her roommate's robe at her, Ellen added pleadingly, "Please Kerry, enjoy my big moment with me."

Beautiful Hong Kong lay before them. Stately ocean liners, blazing with lights and displaying their nation's flags, rose and fell with the rhythm of the waves. Barges, launches and skiffs, loaded with their wares, wove paths of silver foam. Tug boats headed for liners waiting to dock, while scores of weathered Chinese junks hugged the shoreline.

Fascinated, the young women watched until a faint light in the eastern sky sent them scurrying back to their cabin to get ready for the day ahead. And what a day it would prove to be!

The field mission director met the girls at the dock and helped them through customs. Some time later, with the legal work done and Ellen's bags secured, the three climbed into the waiting van.

The Mission headquarters was an ancient, rambling structure, girdled by a wide porch decked with flowers. The compound was surrounded by a high wall partially hidden by a profusion of vegetation.

"Here, let me help you with that." A young man reached for the bag in Ellen's hand.

Ellen whirled around. "Jim!" she gasped as if she would faint.

Jim's hand went out to steady her. "I'm sorry. I didn't mean to startle you." His eyes were holding hers with an intensity that caused Kerry to feel like an intruder. She dropped her gaze, surprised at the revelation of the moment.

Ellen had met Jim Kendell during her first year at Bible college. Jim was an upper class man—good looking, with wavy brown hair and hazel eyes. He was not much taller than Ellen. His broad shoulders and square jaw reminded Kerry of her friend Jack Austin.

At first, Ellen had admired Jim from afar. Then with the passing of time the two became better acquainted, and she, who prided herself on being very level-headed, found herself falling in love.

Jim, on the other hand, was wary. For one thing, he was just getting over rejection. The young lady, for her own reasons, had turned down his proposal, saying that it was best that they just remain good friends. Although Jim was willing to admit to himself that he was very fond of Ellen, he was not ready to take the plunge again so soon. Ellen had tried to keep her feelings hidden.

After his graduation, Jim kept in touch with Ellen and occasionally visited the college. He always sought Ellen out. *A good sign*, Ellen thought wistfully. There were other tell-tale signs as well: the way his eyes lit up with that certain look whenever she appeared, his seeking her company to the exclusion of others, his obvious interest in her activities and a tone of voice that sometimes spoke volumes. It was not until his commissioning for service in Africa that he had bared his heart.

"Ellen, there's something I feel you should know." She saw at once that he was troubled. Jim hesitated. "You know that I will be working with the nomadic Muslims of the Sahara. I want you to know that I never intend to marry. I could never ask any woman to make the sacrifices of such a life." His eyes begged for understanding. Swallowing hard, he thrust out his hand. "Unless God wills otherwise, I guess this is goodbye."

Ellen took his hand. *I'll go with you*, she wanted to cry out, but Jim was not asking. He was saying goodbye! Lifting misty eyes to his she managed, "Goodbye, Jim. God be with you." She could say no more. Turning, she left the room without any inkling of what Jim's decision was costing him.

"How does it happen that you are here in Hong Kong, Jim?" Ellen wanted to know.

"Well, I got cerebral malaria while I was in Africa."

"Oh, how awful!" interrupted Kerry. "That disease is deadly!"

"Yes, well, that was the diagnosis. The doctor said it was touch-and-go for several months. When I got well enough to travel, the Mission flew me home. They do not recommend that I return to Africa."

"Are you saying you are assigned here in Hong Kong?"

"Yes, Ellen. They needed a Greek teacher at the seminary. The former teacher left for furlough, so I'm here to fill the vacancy."

Ellen fought back the flood of excitement that welled up inside. "Well," she said, "you are looking at the new secretary to the Dean of Education at the Seminary."

It was the wee hours of the morning before Ellen and Kerry quieted down. It had been an emotionally exhausting day for Ellen. But Kerry, wide-eyed, tossed and turned, her mind racing on. It would not take a prophet to foretell Ellen's future. But what about hers?

Enough of this, she chided herself. *It will soon be time to get up if I am to get back to the ship by ten o' clock.*

15

It was not easy saying goodbye to Ellen. A few weeks ago they had been total strangers. Now, their friendship ran deep. At the pier their farewells were affectionate and sincere.

Kerry turned and hurried up the gangplank. She turned the key in the cabin lock. As the door pushed open, her eyes fell on Ellen's empty bed. It would be a long, lonely trip to Manila.

Kerry slumped into the chair. *Why this awful feeling of emptiness?* she asked herself. *Was it because of all the recent goodbyes? Maybe, but it was far more than that.* An inner stirring that Kerry thought had been conquered long ago was shattering her contentment with "single blessedness." She had to admit it: she wanted to be married.

Reaching for her well-worn Bible, she flipped it open to Psalm 37:4. "Delight yourself in the Lord and He will give you the desires of your heart." The words brought both comfort and instruction. Yes, she had put her hand to the plow. She would seek God's will above all—whether single or married.

The blast of the ship's whistle jarred Kerry from her reverie. Out on deck she noticed that many ships were cluttering the harbor, among them a gigantic British warship. The cold salt air was rejuvenating. Then suddenly tense-faced seamen were scrambling everywhere. Above the din she heard the captain of the ship bawl out the order: "Drop the anchors!" Realizing that something was very wrong, she saw that the Madison was bearing down on the British ship.

Dear God, we're going to collide! Kerry stood frozen, until an officer nearby shouted, "Lady, run to the other side. Hurry!" Kerry found an iron post, hung on and waited for the impact. But the grinding crunch never came. Just in time, the Madison slowed and then stopped. But so close were the vessels that the ropes on both ships were touching.

Kerry breathed a prayer of thanksgiving. Had she known then what she later learned—that the warship was loaded with explosives—her prayer would have been more fervent by far!

The rest of the day and well into the night the crew worked feverishly to disentangle the anchors, but with no success. Finally the captain ordered that the anchor be severed and left in the harbor. Too much time had been lost already. They were due to dock in Manila in just 36 hours.

"At least this trip can't be described as dull!" someone commented.

That sentiment was to become a prophecy of things to come. This trip was only just the beginning of an anything-but-dull future for Miss Kerry McCormick.

16

Kerry had been informed that she would be met by a missionary of another mission who was located in Manila. He would be responsible for her until she could secure passage on an inter-island steamer going south.

But with all these passengers milling about, how will he ever find me? Kerry wondered. It was a worrisome thought, for she was a total stranger in a strange land. Anxiously she scanned the sea of faces.

Suddenly she noticed a man zigzagging across the room, waving a card with her picture on it. It was one of her prayer cards.

Some thoughtful person had sent it to him for identification purposes.

"Hello there. You must be Miss McCormick?" Kerry nodded and they shook hands warmly. "Welcome to the Philippines! Did you have a nice trip?"

"Yes, except for a few scary moments."

"That seems to be par for the course. I think sometimes the only thing that keeps those old crates afloat are the missionaries on board!" He laughed heartily.

"Thank you for meeting me."

"My pleasure. It is always a joy to welcome new missionaries. We thank God for everyone that comes! And now, shall we get your bags? I'll see what I can do to help you through customs without too much strain on your pocketbook! By the way, I'm Joe Harding, working with the Philippines Bible Society here."

All Kerry's fears were laid to rest by the thoughtfulness of Mr. Harding. She was further relieved when he informed her that she would be staying with him and his wife until her steamer left.

As Kerry's feet touched Philippine soil, little tingles raced up and down her spine. *Thank you, Lord,* she breathed softly. *Thank you for giving me this privilege of serving You here. And O God, please help me serve You well!* It was a prayer from the depth of her heart.

Alice Harding smiled to herself as she noticed their guest eyeing the steaming bowl of rice. McCormicks were Irish. Potatoes were their favorite. Rice had never been served in their home except as dessert. Here in the Philippines, however, rice was their basic food.

"You know how I learned to eat rice?" Alice asked. "I put butter and a little brown sugar on it. Before long I could eat it just as is, and in time, so will you."

Kerry wasn't so sure. This was going to take some adjustment. Just then the house helper carried in a platter of fish and set it down in front of Alice. It was fried to a golden brown, head and all! Kerry stared at it, wide-eyed.

"I know." said Alice noticing the strange look on Kerry's face. "It bothered me too. But Filipinos say the fish head is the most succulent part. Just ignore it and enjoy the rest."

Kerry swallowed hard. "It would be a lot easier if only that eye didn't glare at me so accusingly!" she quipped.

The Hardings joined in the laughter, pleased that this young missionary had a sense of humor. It would no doubt come in very handy.

Kerry had a few problems getting adjusted to Filipino food, but she had no problem appreciating the beauty of her surroundings. The people were attractive and appealing. Sunday morning the men looked immaculate in their barong tagalogs or white coats and ties. The women walked daintily in their colorful mestiza dresses with large butterfly sleeves and creamy sampagita flowers tucked in their raven hair. Everyone was friendly, inclining their heads in greeting and smiling warmly, white teeth sparkling. *It won't be difficult to love these people*, she mused.

The big question was: would she also be able to love the tribespeople of Mindanao, their teeth filed and discolored by the chewing of beetlenut, their skin tattooed and scaly with disease. Only time would tell. Right now, no cloud obscured her horizon. Her hand was on the plow. She would not turn back.

Tuesday morning arrived all too soon. This was the day she would board the S.S. Mayon for the four-day trip to Mindanao

Island. At the dock Joe suggested, "If you get up real early, not later than three, you will be able to see the Southern Cross. This constellation is very clear as one nears the equator." Kerry had read about the Southern Cross and was eager to see it. But three o'clock sounded awfully early!

"Three o'clock?" she exclaimed. Joe laughed, "Unless I miss my guess, it will be a lot easier than you think!"

Kerry soon found out why—everybody slept on deck. The cabins were insufferably hot, so cots were lined up side by side on deck. To get into her cot, Kerry had to hike herself up from the bottom. Sure enough, she found herself wide-awake at the suggested time.

It was a beautiful moonlit night. There was the Southern Cross, high and serene in the sky. "Incredible!" Kerry whispered. "The God of creation has put a cross in the sky!"

The four days on the Mayon passed slowly. She was dismayed to learn when they arrived at Cotobato City that instead of tying up alongside a pier, all passengers would have to transfer from the steamer to a launch which was waiting for them at the mouth of the Cotobato River. The river was too shallow to accommodate the larger ship.

Kerry peered down at the tiny launch, bobbing up and down in the turbulent waters many feet below. "How do we get down there?" she asked.

"Jump," was the reply. "It's okay, we'll help you."

The cargo door swung open and one by one the passengers jumped. Two sturdy seamen, their legs spread-eagled to maintain balance, caught and steadied each one as they landed on the roof of the pitching craft. Kerry made it safely and to her great relief the launch was soon putting down the muddy, crocodile-infested river toward the steamy little town of Cotobato.

17

Kerry created quite a stir. "Have you seen the new missionary yet? Aba! She is young and maganda!" It had been many years since Cotabato had seen such a young and attractive American.

On the upper veranda of the missionary's residence, across from the town plaza, Kerry watched a group of people gathering around a young man who was singing and playing a guitar. The crowd was giggling and looking toward Kerry. The song had something to do with her! The young man was singing a native love ballad! Kerry was being serenaded! Mrs. Wilson, Kerry's hostess, laughingly remarked, "You'll have to be careful, my dear. Filipino young men are very romantic." It was said lightly, but Kerry sensed a veiled warning.

"I'm afraid I have some bad news for you," Bob Wilson's glance rested on Kerry. "I hesitate breaking this to you so soon, but there's been a change of plans."

"Oh, I hope it won't delay our trip to Kidapawan!"

"You won't be going to Kidapawan. Miss Hall has been taken ill and had to leave the station. As you know, she was alone there. She is now in the hospital in Zamboanga City."

"Will she be there long?"

"We don't know." Bob jammed his hands in his pockets and shook his head in disbelief. "She fears she has contracted leprosy." Kerry looked horrified as Bob turned toward the plaza. "It seems that Miss Hall has been working with some lepers. Recently, she noticed a spot on her scalp that wouldn't heal." Turning back to Kerry, he continued, "We are praying for a good medical report. If God in His mercy grants that, we will recommend that she return to the States for a short furlough. In the meantime, we have had to close the station." Kerry opened her mouth to respond but Bob stopped her with an uplifted hand. "You must understand that we can't send you there, a new missionary, without the language, alone."

Kerry was fighting back tears, both for the one who was to have been her co-worker and for her own shattered dreams. Ever since the night the call of God came to her, she believed without a question that she would work with unreached tribespeople. The challenging word of the great Apostle Paul had become her battle cry: "How can they believe in the one of whom they have not heard? And how can they hear without someone preaching to them?" She felt Marj Wilson's arm go across her shoulders and sensed her sympathy even before she spoke. "We're sorry, Kerry, but when God closes one door, He opens another. There's a lot to be done right here!"

Stubbornly Kerry responded. "God's delays are not necessarily His denials, either. I believe He will send me to the tribes yet!"

Of the several young people who were attending the chapel in Cotobato City, Carlos

Mendez was the acknowledged leader. He had all the qualifications: a sharp mind, pleasing personality, speaking skills, and strong motivation. He was a young believer and he was greatly concerned for his family and friends. However, he was not having much success in getting them interested in the gospel. "What could we do to attract your friends," Kerry wondered aloud.

"Well, for starters," Carlos suggested, "how about putting up a pingpong table? Filipinos love to play pingpong. I guarantee that will bring young people in and you will have a captive audience. You can tell them the gospel."

Kerry and the Wilsons made the arrangements while Carlos rounded up his pals. In no time the room was full of enthusiastic young players. As Kerry watched from the sidelines, she thought, "These kids are good. They play hard. But Carlos is by far the best."

Kerry passed around some homemade cookies. To her astonishment, nobody took one. Whoever heard of young people not liking cookies? Kerry put the plate aside.

Somewhat embarrassed, Carlos whispered, "Ma'am, if you will offer three times, we will accept."

Kerry picked up the plate and made the rounds again. Still no takers. Once more she offered. In no time the plate was empty!

After the young people had left, the Wilsons explained. "It's the custom here to wait until an offer is made three times. The first time is considered to be merely an act of politeness. If you are really sincere, you will offer three times."

"That's ridiculous!" exploded Kerry. "Why offer at all if you don't want people to accept?"

"That's good old-fashioned American thinking, but you are in the Philippines now! You see, Filipinos are very hospitable. I have known them to serve visitors while the family went hungry. So they ask themselves: is this a genuine offer, or are they just being polite? They feel that if the offer is made three times, it must be genuine."

"How long did it take you to learn all this?" Kerry asked. "We're still learning after ten years. And, I might add, we're still finding out they usually have a pretty good reason for the things they do!"

Kerry accepted the mild rebuke. "Thanks. The next time 'east meets west,' I'll try not to be so critical."

Marj looked at her husband. "She'll make it."

Bob nodded in Kerry's direction. "Bully for you. Your adjustment to Philippine culture is off to a good start!"

18

One day Carlos announced, "My mother is inviting you to visit her." After several months of hostility on the part of most of the villagers who were staunch supporters of the traditional church, this gesture of friendliness was very heartening.

"Thank you, Carlos," Kerry responded. "Is morning or afternoon the best time?"

"Afternoon, but not before three o'clock. One to two is siesta time. By three it has cooled down a little. By the way, I hope you're observing siesta?"

"Never miss it," laughed Kerry. "That was one of the first things I learned here."

She shrugged her shoulders. "It's just too hot to do anything else!"

At three o'clock that same day Kerry found herself on her way to the Mendez home. It was an imposing structure, befitting the dwelling of the provincial governor and his family. Carlos met her at the door and led her upstairs to a large, airy room which he called their "sala." Kerry surveyed the pleasant surroundings—the attractive rattan furniture, a variety of potted plants, the floor polished to a satin sheen. Carlos explained that the floor was first waxed, then a large coconut, cut in half, was placed on the floor, husk side down and rubbed back and forth. That's what produced the beautiful shine.

"Do you have to get down on your hands and knees?" queried Kerry.

"No, we use our feet. We put one foot on the coconut and push it back and forth while hopping alongside on the other foot. The weight of your body on the coconut husk does the work." Carlos flashed his ready smile. "It's good exercise!"

Rosita Mendez was a large women and as a mother was highly respected in this country where big families were popular. Her brood numbered 10. She seated herself, her round face wreathed in smiles. "I'm glad you've come," she said simply. "My children have been telling me about you, especially this Carlos here. He said you were young and beautiful and you are."

A rosy flush crept over Kerry's face. "Why, thank you, Carlos!" Then, looking back at his mother, she added, "Your son is a fine young man. He's a real help to us at the chapel."

"He's a good boy, and becoming more religious all the time. I often see him sitting here reading his Bible. He's my oldest son, you know, and I count on him to help me with his brothers and sisters."

Carlos was becoming a little uncomfortable. He stood to his feet, "I'll go see about some refreshments."

Kerry turned toward Rosita. "How old is Carlos?"

"Seventeen. He will be finishing high school in a few months. Then he will go to Manila to study law. The governor is insisting on this."

"We will miss him at the chapel when he leaves." Then looking directly at Mrs. Mendez, Kerry said, "I'd like to invite you and the governor to attend our services too."

The woman hesitated. "Sometime, maybe,

but my husband is a politician." Her voice died away to a whisper. "We don't want to lose our friends." From the sadness in her eyes, Kerry got the distinct impression that the sentiment expressed the views of her husband, not her own.

"I just want you to know that you are both welcome anytime," Kerry said gently. "And thank you for letting your children come."

"Oh, I can see it is doing them good," Mrs. Mendez replied. Then, turning her head, she called out, "Carlos, the merienda."

The long, cool drink of calamunsi was refreshing, but soon it was time to leave. Kerry extended her hand and looked deep into the misty eyes of the older woman. They betrayed both longing and fear.

"Carlos will see you to the door. I hope you will come again soon!"

It's a beginning, thought Kerry, as she made her way down the hot, dusty road, *and with God all things are possible!*

The screech of bicycle wheels on the gravel behind her brought Kerry to attention. She had come down to the pier to watch the sunset and as ever was captivated by the beauty filling sea and sky. Now the colors were fading, but still she sat there, lost in thought.

"You startled me, Carlos. My mind was many miles away."

He looked at her accusingly. "I saw you leave your house alone."

"So? I like to sit alone."

"But it's not good," he broke off, biting his lip.

Kerry's brow wrinkled into a frown. Ignoring that, he went on. "Here, ladies never travel alone even in daytime. It's our custom."

"That word again," groaned Kerry.

"You should always have a companion."

"Why?"

"It's our custom and it isn't safe!"

"But I'm used to being alone. I'm not . . ." With an imperious wave of his hand, he silenced her.

"I don't mean to be disrespectful. I know you are older than I and a missionary. But our people will not understand. I hope you will not do it again."

Kerry could not believe what she was hearing. *This kid telling me what I can and can't do!* But along with stirrings of anger came a warning bell that brought back the back the words of Bob Wilson: "We're learning they usually have good reason for the things they do."

"And where do you suggest I get a companion? I can't asked Mrs. Wilson to accompany me everywhere I go!"

"It doesn't have to be an adult. A child, anyone. Please."

"Oh, okay," she answered curtly. "I won't go out alone at night, but I make no promises for daytime. I have a job to do and I can't let the lack of a companion interfere."

"You're angry," Carlos retorted.

Getting up from her perch on the pier and brushing off the dust, Kerry faced him. "I guess I am a little angry. I'm also bewildered, and, to be perfectly frank, afraid that I'll never be able to make the adjustments that I know I must make." The tears were close to the surface. "Thanks, Carlos. I really am grateful for your concern. I can use a friend!"

Carlos smiled. "I'll be that friend or die trying!"

19

The two women hesitated outside the big wooden gate.

"Are you sure this is the mission house, Lucia?" asked Gregoria.

"I'm sure. Do you still want to go in?"

"If you do. But what will we say to the missionary?"

"Tell her we want to learn the Word of God but we are old and can't read. How can we learn if we can't read?"

Gregoria's grey head nodded vigorously. "And will she please come and teach a Bible class in my house? Do you think she will come?"

"There's only one way to find out—ask her!" Lucia placed both bony hands on the gate and gave a determined push. Slowly the gate creaked open.

Kerry greeted the women at the door and invited them in. Both seemed uncomfortable and shy, but the missionary's warm smile and gentle manner put them at ease. Haltingly they presented their request. Kerry's heart gave a responsive leap. She had met with so many rebuffs of late—people avoiding her or openly hostile. But here were two women waiting to be taught!

"Indeed I will come and teach you! Are you living in town?"

"We are from Upi, about an hour's bus ride from here."

"In the mountains, where the Tirurays live," added Gregoria.

"Upi? Is that where the recent uprisings have been?"

"Yes, but it's peaceful now. You can get back here before sundown."

"When do you want to start? This week?"

Lucia's black eyes shone. "Oh, thank you, Mum. Any time you say."

Kerry set out to find someone to go with her. Marj Wilson questioned the wisdom of going at this time. "The tribespeople living there have been angered because of a requirement from the government for military training. When they protested, one of their villages was burned and consequently they are sharpening their bolos and spears."

"That's scary! What happened?"

"A band of thirty to fifty rode down the mountain and murdered several lowlanders, then hid in the mountains."

"And they're still hiding?"

"That's what I hear. I understand armed government soldiers are on every bus going there. But we have not heard of any incidents lately. Things do seem to have quieted down."

"The women said it was safe now. They are so eager to have me come. I would not want to disappoint them."

"Well, do what you have to do. I'll ask Lucinda if she will go with you. She's a brave little soul—nothing scares her."

The rickety bus to Upi lumbered over twisting, ever ascending mountain road and, to Kerry's great relief, reached its destination safely. Lucia met them and escorted them to Gregoria's thatch-roofed one-room house. As Kerry entered she noticed that others were there too, among them an old, shrunken woman, crippled, wasted and with a hacking cough. *Why, she must be a hundred years old*, thought Kerry, *too old, no doubt, to really understand. Perhaps for her the gospel has come too late.*

The lesson was based on the third chapter of John. Very simply Kerry pointed out God's wonderful love in sending His Son into the world to die for the sins of all mankind. She emphasized the resurrection of Jesus Christ. She wasn't sure how much was being understood, but she encouraged her listeners to receive the gift God had promised. "Whoever comes to me, I will never drive away" (John 6:37).

As Kerry bowed her head to close in prayer, the withered woman began to pray, asking God to save her. Her prayer over, she looked into Kerry's face and smiled. "Such wonderful news you brought us, that salvation is a gift of God! I'm very old and if I had to work for salvation there would be no hope for me!"

The Bible study was like a shot in the arm to Kerry. She determined to return at least once a month. The youth work in town was also expanding, largely through the efforts of the young people themselves.

One morning early, before the cool of the

night gave way to blistering heat, Kerry went to the market to buy some dried fish. The vendor found her request very amusing. Smiling broadly, with a white toothy grin, she exclaimed, "Aba! Americans eat dried fish?"

"I don't know about others, but I do," Kerry responded. "When I was growing up, we ate dried herring every New Year's Eve. I really like it!"

At this, the vendor laughed again. "You are like Filipino already! My son tell me you want to learn our ways."

"Your son? Do I know him?"

"He is Felipe. He goes to your chapel to play pingpong and to hear you teach the Bible."

"Felipe is your son? Then you are Mrs. Villegas! Filipe has told me about you."

Mrs. Villegas sniffed. "He is perhaps telling you about how I am always wearing brown, no?" She looked at Kerry quizzically, then went on. "He hates it, but I am wearing it because of my vow to Saint Carmen." As soon as the words were out, her expression changed. Frowning, she bit her lip and lowered her gaze.

"Is something wrong?" Kerry's face

registered concern. The woman replied, "I am all right, but have very big problem."

Kerry's heart went out to her. When she spoke her voice was gentle. "I know Someone Who can help you with your problem. His name is Jesus."

Abruptly, Mrs. Villegas turned away to wait on another customer. But as Kerry prepared to leave, she heard her say, "I come talk to you soon."

The meeting took place that very same night. Under cover of darkness, Mrs. Villegas appeared at Kerry's door.

Once inside the house, she spoke forthrightly, "Miss . . . ?"

"Call me Kerry."

"Good. I have trouble with long name." Smiling nervously, she hurried on. "I am religious woman, but have sinned a great sin!" She waited for Kerry's reaction, but Kerry was too busy asking God to give her wisdom to react to the woman's confession.

Mrs. Villegas continued, "Three years ago, before this one was born," indicating baby Jasmine who was sound asleep on her mother's shoulder, "my youngest child died. She was buried in the cemetery by the church. But we are very poor and have no money to pay for renting the graves. We cannot keep up and time goes by and we do not pay. I am so afraid my baby's bones will be removed and the grave given to another."

Kerry gasped. "Surely they would not do that!"

"Someone warned me that they will." Big tears rolled down the thin cheeks. Wringing her work-worn hands she blurted out, "One night—it was very dark—I go to the cemetery and dig up the small coffin and bring it home. Since then, I do not go to church. I am afraid to confess my sin."

Putting her arm around the sobbing woman, Kerry said gently, "Mrs. Villegas, you don't have to be afraid to go directly to Christ and confess your sins. He loves you and died for you and He will answer your prayer."

"Do you think I can ask Him now, here?" A ray of hope shone in the red-rimmed eyes.

"Yes! He wants you to come. Believe me, He will not turn you away!"

Very simply Mrs. Villegas prayed, asking God for cleansing and salvation. When her prayer was over, she placed her hand over her heart. "Here I feel so clean. The blood of Jesus has made me so clean!"

20

A lively game was in progress when Kerry entered the room. She was so intrigued with the agility and skillfulness of the players that she failed to notice the stranger who stood watching her.

"Bravo!" she shouted, as a powerful back drive ended the game. Carlos, the victor, grinning from ear to ear, fanned himself with the racket. Then making his way to the newcomer, he welcomed him with a friendly handshake. Together they approached Kerry.

"Miss McCormick, this is Solocan Napila, a former student in our high school here. I met him in town today and found out he wasn't busy tonight, so I invited him to join us. He used to play a mean game of pingpong!"

Kerry was instantly struck by the appearance of the stranger. He was tall, taller than most Filipino men, and muscular. He had a wide engaging smile, but it was his eyes that held her—black and piercing. A somewhat haughty bearing set him apart. "I'm glad you could join us, Solocan. We are just about to begin our Bible study. Please feel free to stay. We would be glad to have you."

"Thank you," his deep voice resonated. All the while, his eyes revealed open admiration. Kerry felt uncomfortable. *Obviously not shy!* she thought, then dismissed him from her mind and signaled Carlos to begin the meeting.

Long after the meeting had ended, Kerry reflected on the words of Solocan. He had joined in as the young people voiced their prayer requests.

"Some of you know me, but for those who do not, I am a Bilaan from Sarangani. There is no one in my area to teach us about God. My people are spirit-worshippers. My request is that someone will come and teach us the Bible. As the son of the chief of the Bilaan tribe, I will welcome them."

He sat down and from the hush that descended on the room it was clear his appeal had sobered the group. As for Kerry, she seemed to hear once more the words of the missionary of years gone by: "How can they believe in the one of whom they have not heard? And how can they hear without someone preaching to them?" Her response, though not verbalized, was instantaneous, *Here I am Lord, send me.*

Before retiring to her room, Kerry sought out the Wilsons. "Do you remember Solocan Napila? He attended high school here several years ago."

Marj wrinkled her brow. "Solocan Napila? I have heard the name."

"He's a Bilaan from Sarangani."

"Oh yes, a tall fellow. He came to the mission a few times. We thought him a little strange. The young people called him wild and savage."

"Savage? He seemed civilized enough to me. Bold perhaps, but civilized."

"He was here tonight?"

"Carlos brought him and he said something I haven't been able to forget."

"Oh?"

"He wants someone to go to his people and teach them the Bible."

"And I suppose you're ready to volunteer?"

"There's nothing I would like better if I was sure it was the leading of the Lord."

"Well, you'll have plenty of time to find out. The mission would never send a single new missionary alone and I don't know if there is anyone available to go with you. Let's ask Bob."

Bob's reply was not encouraging. "No one at present. The only possibility would be Marion Roberts."

"But she's been working among the Monobos," interjected Marj.

"Yes. It's a long shot all right. She may not feel her work there is finished. Besides she's home on furlough just now and we haven't had any word from her as to when to expect her back."

In the weeks that followed, Kerry did not permit her continuing interest in the Bilaans to interfere with responsibilities in Cotobato. Then, one day a letter came from Marion Roberts. Excitedly the Wilsons shared it with Kerry. "My sailing date is May 10. I should be there in early June."

Kerry was elated. Bob was excited too.

"This might work out after all, Kerry. Marion is a real pioneer and if she is interested at all in the Bilaans, you're in business."

It turned out that Marion Roberts was indeed interested in the Bilaans. She was a warm-hearted, middle-aged woman with years of experience in tribal work among the Monobos, then the Bogobos and now on to the Bilaans. So it was settled. Kerry would accompany the older missionary to this brand new pioneer field.

When it came right down to leaving Cotobato, Kerry's heart was torn. It was not easy to say goodbye to Mrs. Villegas and Mrs. Mendez. It was not easy to leave her Bible class in Upi and the host of young people that she had come to love. Judging from their tears, they were sorry to see her go too. On the day of their departure, they trooped to the pier, many bringing farewell gifts in their hands—lovely orchid plants, Filipino delicacies, even a saucy parrot. Carlos' gift was a cute little puppy which Kerry immediately scooped up in her arms and dubbed "Pal."

Too soon the launch loosed its moorings and headed to the open sea, where the inter-island steamer awaited them.

21

Bob Wilson had preceded the ladies to Glan to secure housing. He managed to find a dwelling which, unlike the native one-room cogon-roofed shacks, was a wooden structure with a tin roof. It was elevated about three feet off the ground, with a bamboo ladder for steps.

Outside, two large drums stood on a rustic shelf, catching rain water off the roof. This would be the only source of clean water—the alternative being the muddy river at the edge of town which served as public bath and laundry for the entire village.

Besides the kitchen, there were three small rooms with plank floors, a larger sala and an outhouse. The kitchen was tiny and completely bare of furnishings except for the charcoal stove and a narrow ledge with a drainboard made of wooden slats. The floor of the kitchen was split bamboo, with narrow spaces between each strip.

Marian Roberts was pleased with the provision. "I brought along some material for curtains," she said, "and with our potted plants, a table or two and some chairs, it will be quite liveable! We'll have somebody make us a bench for the sala, and then of course we'll have your pump organ."

At the moment, Kerry did not share her enthusiasm. "What about snakes and rats? Everything is open!" she quaked.

"And centipedes and scorpions and black-widow spiders!" added Marian. "They're all here, but our mosquito nets will keep them out while we sleep. When we're up and about, keep a sharp eye! And never go outside without a flash light. Snakes, you know."

Kerry's stricken look caused Marion to quickly change the subject. "Now, how about a cup of tea? We'll feel more like unpacking after tea and biscuits."

The tea kettle and cups were soon located. Marian was an old hand at lighting a charcoal stove, so before long the tea kettle was singing. Perched on a trunk, she raised her steaming cup in a toast: "Here's to our new home, Kerry. May it ever be a place of . . . " Suddenly she broke off, jumped down from the trunk, reached for the tea kettle and dumped some water between the bamboo slats. From under the house came a muffled cry and the sounds of scrambling. Marian picked up her cup again and, winking broadly, announced, "That should help discourage unwanted visitors!"

By nightfall, both women were exhausted. The tropical sun beating down on the roof had made the house an oven. But their hard work had paid off. The place was beginning to take on the semblance of a home.

Before Kerry dropped off to sleep, she did something that would become a habit every day and every night following: she commited herself to the safe keeping of her Savior. "For he will command his angels concerning you to guard you in all your ways," she murmured drowsily, quoting Psalm 91:11.

For one brief moment her mind flew to snakes and centipedes and scorpions and unwanted visitors. But soon she was asleep.

22

Breakfast was scarcely over before Solocan made his appearance. He was apologetic. "I see I'm interrupting. Guess I'm too eager to get started. Sorry."

"No, no, we're finished. Get started on what?" Marian, whom Kerry now simply called "Ann," was puzzled.

"Your language study." Solocan turned piercing eyes upon her. "You won't be able to do much without the language of my people."

"Yes, of course," she said nodding at Kerry. "We have talked about that. Do you know anyone we could get to teach us?"

The chief's son spoke with emphasis. "I'm afraid you ladies are stuck with me." His words were spoken to Ann, but his eyes rested on Kerry. The arrangement made Kerry nervous.

"Surely there must be others here who speak English?" Kerry questioned. Then, realizing how unthankful she sounded, she added hastily, "I mean, you must be very busy."

"Not too busy to be of help," Solocan answered curtly. Then, in a modified tone, "I will be happy to teach you my dialect."

"Great!" burst in Ann. "When do we begin?"

"As soon as you are ready."

"We'll have to wait until our helpers get here. They will arrive on the next trip of the Mayon. They reminded us many times to be sure to meet the boat. You can be sure we will."

Satisfied, Solocan left. As soon as he was out of earshot, Ann turned to Kerry. "What was all that about?"

Kerry smiled weakly. "How to win friends and influence people, eh? But I just can't help it! That man makes me uncomfortable. I just wish he wasn't our teacher."

"But we've got to learn the dialect so, like

he said, it seems we're stuck with him even if he is a little overbearing."

"A little!" snorted Kerry, rolling her eyes heavenward, "Wow! You can say that again!"

True to their word, Maria Gonzalez and Rosa Sanchez, the missionaries' helpers, were on board when the Mayon put into port. They had no trouble spotting the two pale faces in a sea of brown. Ann and Kerry welcomed them warmly and escorted them to the room they would share. The girls were happy and excited, so excited that they forgot all about the letters they had been asked to deliver. For Kerry, there were three: one from her sister Tracy, one from Carlos and one from a certain Dr. Peter Cameron. Kerry glanced at this letter, scowling in perplexity. "Strange," Kerry muttered, "I don't know any Dr. Cameron." She opened Tracy's letter first.

"We're all fine here," it read. "Beth's in love—again! But this time I have a feeling it's the real thing! (I guess I'm doomed to be an old maid like you! Ha!) Tom's youngest is adorable—looks just like his proud daddy. Tim's wife is expecting. They're hoping for a boy. Daddy's fine physically, but hasn't yielded to the Lord yet. We know he's doing a lot of thinking. Sue's still keeping the home fires burning, and me—I love my job, have gained five pounds (!!!) and am missing you an awful lot! We all are!" The rest of the letter was a blur as Kerry blinked to keep back tears. She reached for Dr. Cameron's letter.

"Well, for goodness sake, what do you know!" Kerry exclaimed. Ann looked up from the letter she was reading.

"What's up? Anything exciting?"

"Dr. Cameron is a step brother of Jim Kendell!"

"You don't say! And who, may I ask, is Jim Kendell?"

"Jim is the new husband of my friend and cabin-mate, Ellen. I think I mentioned to you that they are working in Hong Kong." Ann nodded. Kerry continued, "Dr. Cameron says Jim gave him my name."

"What for?"

"This man says he is an anthropologist, presently working among the Bontocs in Luzon province. He says he is interested in doing research among the tribes here in Mindanao."

"You mean he wants to come here?"

"Well, he is asking for information. Says he would appreciate any information we could give him. Maybe I ought to put him in touch with the chief's son."

"Ah-h-h, hold on a minute. I don't know if that would be wise. The Bilaans are very backward and Solocan is a proud man. He might not appreciate a foreigner poking his nose into Bilaan culture. But this Dr. Cameron could be a real help to us."

"You think I ought to invite him?"

Ann jumped to her feet, her letter forgotten. "By all means! We could even board him if nothing else turns up."

Kerry looked at Ann. "Board him? In these crowded quarters?"

Ann shook her head, "Oh, I don't mean he would sleep here!" With a knowing wink she continued. "If these people are anything like the Monobos, they would be certain we were his wives! No. That's out. But we could give him his meals and in return he could share some of his research findings with us. It could be interesting."

"But where would he stay in this village of grass huts?"

"I'm not sure. He must have experienced some pretty primitive living among the Bontocs, wouldn't you think?" Ann snapped her fingers. "I have an idea. The Philippine Constabulary in town. They have several buildings. Maybe they would rent him a room."

"Worth looking into. Then I'll write him and tell him to come?"

"Does he say when he would like to come?"

"Not right away, according to this. He says it will take several months to wrap things up there."

"That will give us plenty of time to take care of the details. Yes, get the letter off, Kerry. We need all the help we can get."

Kerry lost no time in answering Dr. Cameron. *Wonder what he's like?* she mused. *Wonder if he's anything like Jim?*

Hundreds of miles away, a certain anthropologist pushed back a stubborn lock of blond hair and muttered, "Sure hope I get a response from Ellen's friend. If I do, my baby brother will have done me a big favor!"

23

Early the following morning, Kerry awoke with a sense of foreboding. Rubbing the sleep from eyes she suddenly remembered—today, language class would begin. Kerry was not looking forward to language study. She already resented the teacher. And how do you learn a language without any help? Bilaan was an unwritten language, so there was no grammar, no books of any kind. Well, she'd have to make the best of it. She had no option. The dialect had to be learned.

In her devotions that morning, Kerry prayed, "Dear Lord, I'm glad I don't have to tackle this alone. You have promised to be with me and so far You have never failed. I know you will not fail me now."

From the very start, Ann, who had already learned the Monobo and Bogodo dialects, showed herself a much more apt pupil than Kerry. Wearily, Kerry focused her attention on the teacher. *Watch his mouth*, she cautioned herself sternly. *Notice the position of his lips.* But try as she did, language study was proving to be more difficult than she had imagined. When Solocan suggested that each one be taught privately, Kerry balked. But Ann, who had chafed a bit at Kerry's slow progress, agreed. The thought of being alone with Solocan made Kerry uneasy, but she had to admit that dividing the class was more fair to Ann.

Classes continued without incident. Kerry was beginning to relax a bit. She was actually improving in her study. Now if she could only find a native to practice her slow, faltering speech on.

Kerry often went to the market place to look for help, but with no success. Far from conversing with her, the women only stared, fear evident in their eyes.

"They act like they're afraid of me," she

complained to Solocan. He nodded his head knowingly. "The witch doctor has scared them. He is circulating a rumor that you missionaries have a plan to kidnap Bilaans and sell them to a man having golden horns! The witch doctor can be very convincing."

One day at the market, however, a woman edged up to Kerry and smiled reassuringly. No words were spoken, but Kerry thought: *With time, the wall of silence will disappear. Please God, let it be soon!*

24

Maria plunked her shopping basket down on the kitchen table, struggling to catch her breath. She had been running—running scared! Seeing the missionaries were in the sala, she shrieked, "It's Solocan. We have to get out of here right away!"

Ann headed for Maria and, taking her by the shoulders, shook her firmly. "What is it, Maria? What happened?"

The words tumbled out. "Solocan . . . in the market . . . I heard him say he was going to kill the missionaries!"

Ann and Kerry looked at each other.

Maria continued, "That's what he said. I heard him. Oh please, let's go now!"

Kerry jumped to her feet and, placing her arm around the thin, heaving shoulders, said quietly, "God won't let him harm us, Maria. Remember our Bible verse this morning, 'do not fear, for I am with you.' By the way, where is Rosa?"

"Washing clothes—at the river."

Gently Kerry steered Maria toward the door. "Maybe she could use your help." As soon as Maria was out of earshot, Kerry flashed, "This is unbelievable! Has Solocan lost his mind?"

Ann was skeptical. "More likely he is trying to frighten us for some reason, trying to scare us away."

"But why? He's the one who invited us here!"

"I know, but don't forget we invaded the enemy's territory. Satan is sure to put up a fight. There will be opposition."

"But from our language teacher?" Kerry broke in.

"It's hard to believe this about Solocan. He speaks English and dresses in Western-style clothes, but his background was, and maybe still is, demon worship. If he is under the control of Satan, who knows what the devil will put in his mind?"

"Are you saying he might try to carry out his threat?"

Ann shook her head. "I really don't think so. For one thing, I think he intended Maria to hear the threat and knew she would report it to us. If he really wanted to harm us, does it seem likely he would warn us ahead of time?"

Kerry brightened. "That makes sense. I sure hope you're right. It was just a scare tactic."

"However," Ann added seriously, "the fact remains that Solocan may prove to be a formidable foe. We must take care."

"If God be for us, who can be against us?" quoted Kerry, her voice ringing with confidence.

"Exactly!" Kerry's fervor was contagious. "Because of the cross and the empty tomb we are on the winning side!"

Solocan did not show up for the next lesson, or the next, or the next. Apart from that, life went on as usual.

One morning, Ann was off to the market bright and early. They had learned that the earlier the better, for produce was scarce. There was always an abundance of fish, but vegetables were limited to camotes, long thin string beans, short, fat cooking bananas called saba, and rice. And there were open kegs of unrefined sugar where flies swarmed in great numbers. Chickens and eggs were scarce and milk non-existent except for coconut milk. Fortunately, they were able to order supplies from the lowlands to supplement their diet—things like canned milk, canned meats, and tea.

Kerry turned her attention to watering her treasured orchids. Water from the river seemed to damage the delicate blossoms, so precious rain water was used. To conserve the water, she dipped a cupful out of a small pail, poured it on the plant and, holding the pail under the plant, waited until every unused drop of the liquid drained back.

As Kerry worked at a window opposite the door, she suddenly had a strange feeling. Was there a snake, perhaps a cobra, in the room? Only a few days earlier she watched a native kill a cobra right in front of their house, so she knew the deadly reptiles were around.

Kerry whirled around. Her eyes looked right into the distorted face of Solocan! He had slipped in noiselessly in his bare feet.

And now, he was up on his tiptoes, his arm raised, a long-handled axe in his hand.

Kerry stood frozen, but made no sound for she was keenly aware of the presence of Another, Jesus Christ, her Savior and Lord. Her unexpected calm seemed to unnerve Solocan. Lowering the axe, he started swinging it toward her, his muscles rippling, his eyes wild and dilated.

Kerry's body pressed tightly against the window. She could back up no further. Each rapid sweep of the blade, back and forth, back and forth, was missing her by scarcely an inch. Abruptly Solocan stopped swinging. "If you hadn't looked when you did, I would have chopped your neck!" In a flash, he was gone.

The whole incident took only a few minutes but, for Kerry, time stood still. Feeling faint, she reached for a chair and collapsed into it. Slowly, in a trembling voice the words came, "Dear Lord Jesus, thank You for being here just like You promised."

25

Ann listened in stunned silence as Kerry related her experience with Solocan. All she could say was, "How awful, how awful for you." Walking over to Kerry, she placed a comforting hand on her bowed head. "I'm so sorry. I was so terribly wrong. He does intend harm!" Turning, she began to pace the room, pausing once more in front of Kerry to say, "Now we have a problem. What are we going to do? We must do something."

Kerry looked up at the veteran missionary and blurted, "If I did what I feel like doing, I'd get out of here, fast!"

Ann nodded. "We may have to do that. It's a sure thing we can't help the Bilaans if we're dead!"

Timidly Kerry asked, "But how can we leave? We were so sure the Lord sent us here."

Ann ceased her pacing and returned to her chair. "That's what we have to settle. Do we know that for a certainty? Did we come out of sympathy for this neglected tribe or did we come in obedience to God's call?"

Kerry, was silent for a moment. Then meeting Ann's steady gaze, she spoke firmly. "I can't answer for you, Ann, but as for me, I believe God led me here. Are you questioning God's leading?"

"Not for a moment."

"Then?"

"Then what?"

"Since He led us here, to leave now would be getting out of His will."

Ann clasped her hands together. "Oh, how I wanted to hear you say that! So?"

"Since we know He lead us here . . . "

"Yes?"

"He will take care of us." Smiling warmly, Kerry added, "My pastor often said, 'the safest place in all the world is the center of the will of God.' "

"It's settled then. We stay?"

"We stay and get on with the job the Lord sent us here to do."

Ann's smile washed over Kerry like a benediction. "Spoken like a real trouper, young lady. Bully for you!"

26

The following days brought some changes. Number one on the agenda was to find a new language teacher. Kerry and Ann learned of a young man, Sabid by name, who could speak some English and who might be willing to help them.

He was willing—for a sum. So language study continued. Before long both missionaries had advanced far enough with the dialect that they could begin thinking about holding Bible classes. Sabid would act as interpreter. Passages from the Bible needed to be translated in Bilaan, but since Sabid had never come in contact with the scripture, his understanding was very limited. Finding the right word to express a Bible truth was often tedious.

Concerned about Sabid's spiritual needs, Kerry chose First John 1:9 as the first verse of study: "If we confess our sins, he is faithful and just and will forgive our sins, and purify us from all unrighteousness." Sabid did fairly well until he came to the word "forgive."

"What's forgive?" he asked. Ann explained as best she could. Sabid's brow wrinkled. "We Bilaans do not understand forgive. We have no word for that. If someone wrongs us, we get revenge. I cannot give you a word for forgive."

Each class was started by prayer. That always disturbed Sabid. His eyes would dart all over the room in an effort to see the spirits the missionaries were talking to. One day Sabid remarked, "We believe in spirits, one good, many bad. We call on them to curse our enemies. We do not fear the good spirit. He will not harm us. But we offer sacrifices to the bad spirits so they will not make us sick and will give us a good harvest."

Kerry was incredulous. "You know about the Good Spirit?" she asked.

Sabid inclined his head. "We know someone put that mountain there," he said with a sweep of his hand, "and that forest. But we don't know His Name."

"His Name is Jesus Christ," whispered Kerry, her voice choked with emotion. "We want to tell you about Him." Thus began the witness to Sabid. It took many weeks before the truth gripped him.

"How long have you known this Jesus?" Sabid wanted to know.

Kerry hesitated for a brief moment. "I . . . I really didn't know Him, but, I have known about Him since . . . well, since I was a little girl."

"Did your mother know about Him?"

"Yes." It was not more than a whisper.

Sabid, gazing out of the window said sadly, "We Bilaans are like that banana plant. The old leaves are gone, destroyed. We are new shoots and to us this good news of Jesus has come." Turning from the window, he looked at Kerry accusingly, "Why didn't you come sooner?"

A flush rose over the missionary's pale face. His words pierced her heart. "I'm so sorry your people have waited so long. But we're here now and you must help us reach your people."

Sabid nodded assent. "Do you think you could climb the mountain to my village?"

"I'll sure try," Kerry ventured.

Sabid's eyes shone with excitement. "You must take your bed mat, maybe a little rice and dried fish. We can sleep in my brother's house. It is bigger than mine. And . . . and please, can we take the papers with the pictures of Jesus?"

"The Sunday School charts? Yes, certainly, if you think they will help."

God was opening up a way to share the gospel with a people that had never heard His name. Sabid was thrilled.

27

Ann flopped down in a chair and, throwing her feet up on a bench, grinned broadly. Her eyes danced with excitement.

"Let me guess. You've just won a million dollars!"

"Better than that! I have just been invited to join Lieutenant Castro and his wife for a trip to Dadiangas!" Ann beamed.

Dadiangas was a small settlement across Sarangani Bay where lowlanders from the north were arriving by the boat loads. The government had offered them a small tract of land, a water buffalo, a nipa hut and some food supplies if they would settle in the fertile valley and farm the land. Most of these people came from crowded cities where they could scarcely eke out a living. The offer seemed too good to be true. Ann was glad for the opportunity to go there.

Kerry was as enthusiastic as Ann. "That's great! How will you go?" Kerry wanted to know. "Not by vinta, I hope."

Ann stood up and put on a little strut. "In the comfortable government launch reserved only for VIPS!" Kerry giggled as Ann continued. "Seriously. The lieutenant has to go there on business. He said they will return tonight but warned me it will be late. How about it? Should I go?"

"By all means. Just wish I were going with you. But that's out of the question. One of us has to be here with the girls."

That evening, as Kerry sat down to her evening meal, thoughts of home and loved ones crowded in. She could hear Maria and Rosa chatting in the kitchen. But she was totally alone. Her meal lay before her untouched. Battling back tears she chided herself, *So you're lonely and there isn't a thing you can do about it!* Jumping up from the table, she carried her plate back into the kitchen. Maria looked at the untouched food. "Why, Mum? Are you feeling sick?"

"Just a little homesick, maybe. Sorry about your nice supper. I'm not hungry."

She was not quite out of earshot as she overheard Rosa say, "I think she's lonely. She needs a husband. Then she not be lonely...."

Now that's a happy thought, mused Kerry, *but there's a fat chance I will ever find the man of my dreams out here in the boondocks!*

Later that evening, the three young women gathered in the sala for their devotions. The sun had gone down and a cool breeze wafted in from the open window. This was the time of day Kerry loved best. Dim flickering lights appeared in the village. The only noise was the distant barking of dogs.

Kerry opened her Bible, her loneliness forgotten. Suddenly, without warning, the outside door opened and a man stood framed in the doorway. "May I come in?" he asked.

Seeing Solocan, Kerry's heart gave a leap. A silent desperate plea for help ascended. Struggling to control her voice she answered, "Yes, come in. You're just in time for Bible study and prayer."

Solocan looked embarrassed and chastened. He sat down. Kerry began reading, "Let not your hearts be troubled. Trust in God; trust also in me. In my Father's house are many rooms; if it were not so I would have told you. I am going there to prepare a place for you" (John 14:1). Kerry read until she came to verse 27: "Peace I leave with you; my peace I give you. . . . Do not let your hearts be troubled and do not be afraid."

Customarily, after reading the Bible, the group knelt to pray. Tonight Kerry hesitated, thinking, *Maybe I better not kneel. Maybe I better watch and pray!* But kneel she did. Out of the corner of her eye she saw that Solocan was kneeling too. "Dear Father, . . . " Kerry began. A loud thump interupted her in mid-sentence. Solocan had thrown himself full length on the floor! He was writhing, tearing savagely at his clothes and crashing his elbows on the boards of the floor as he rolled.

Kerry stayed on her knees, glued to the spot. All she could say was, "Lord Jesus, help!" The two girls rushed over to the window, ready to jump. Kerry's impulse was to get up and run too. But suddenly the sweet sense of Christ's presence filled the room.

She watched as Solocan leaped to his feet and strode over to where she was kneeling. "It's no use, missionary, it's no use. Your God can't help me. I'm too wicked."

Kerry's heart went out to Solocan in his agony. Earlier she would have been paralyzed, but now the words came flowing out, "Oh, but you're wrong, Solocan. My God can help you. It was for sinners that Jesus Christ died! He said, 'I have not come to call the righteous, but sinners.' "

By some miracle, the words got through to Solocan. His muscles relaxed and, sinking into a chair, he stared at Kerry as she talked. "The Bible says, 'Though your sins are like scarlet, they shall be as white as snow.' And look at this verse."

Rising to her feet Kerry pointed out the First Epistle of John, verse seven of chapter one, "The blood of Jesus, his Son, purifies us from every sin." And again, "If we confess our sins, he is faithful and just and will forgive us our sins and purify us from all unrighteousness."

In that moment, as Kerry read the verse, God delivered Solocan from the power of darkness. Solocan was now a child of God.

"As long as I can remember," Solocan admitted, "I have been driven by dark powers. But the moment I cried out to Jesus, the darkness fled!"

The light of God's Word had penetrated the blackness and gloom of a pagan heart.

A new day was dawning in Bilaan country.

28

Ann was still sleeping soundly when Kerry and Maria took off for the pier. Each week one of the missionaries met the incoming inter-island steamer, hoping to purchase a pound of butter from the ship's purser. And added to this was the music which often wafted from the ship's radio. Today, Kerry was not disappointed. A rich male voice was singing Joyce Kilmer's "Trees," a song Kerry loved. She stood immobile, lost in the beauty of the voice as well as the lyrics. A sob caught in her throat and stinging tears threatened to spill over. The truth was: Kerry was starved for music! Neither she nor Ann possessed a radio and the only music the Bilaan's knew was a rhythm beaten out on gongs or a monotone chant that completely unnerved her.

Too soon the song ended and the spell was broken. Right then and there she decided that she would teach the Bilaans to sing! A few simple choruses, a hymn or two—she could hardly wait to get started.

Kerry was jolted into reality by the appearance of an unusual passenger. He was an American, certainly not old, of medium height, lean and with blond hair that glinted in the sun. As he made his way down the gangplank he waved and flashed a friendly smile. A thought darted like an arrow to her heart.

"Miss McCormick, how good of you to meet me!"

Kerry stared, not even noticing the hand the stranger had extended in greeting. "You didn't get my letter? I was afraid of that."

Kerry regained her equilibrium. Smiling a brief, uncertain smile, she answered apologetically, "For a moment you lost me. Dr. Cameron, I presume?"

"Forgive my stupidity! Yes, I am Jim's brother—Peter, in the Bible, Hurlburt, for the famous Bible teacher, and Cameron, for my favorite father."

"I see," said Kerry. "And does Peter Hurlburt Cameron always arrive unexpectedly?"

"Let me explain. I finished my work in the mountain provinces, then dashed off to Manila and mailed you a letter from there. I knew I was taking a chance on it beating me here." Peter looked embarrassed.

Kerry laughed. "It's okay. Your letter will probably arrive today. You see, we have no airfield, no roads, and this boat comes in from the north only once a week. But no matter," she added breezily, "we have your accommodations ready. I should have guessed the American was you. But you don't look a bit like your brother Jim."

Peter laughed good-naturedly. "Jim favors our mother. We have different dads, you know, and I favor my dad." Then, his fine eyes crinkling with amusement, he added, "You're not exactly what I expected, either," he continued. "Jim did say a lot of nice things about you, but he forgot to add 'pretty'!"

Kerry's color heightened. She managed a faint thank you, and then, clearing her throat, announced, "It isn't far to your quarters. Can we give you a hand with some of these things?"

"Thanks, but I can manage." With Kerry leading the way, they soon arrived at the constabulary grounds where Peter was introduced to the lieutenant. Before leaving, Kerry made sure that Peter knew he was invited for lunch.

"I'll be there. And thanks for everything." As Kerry turned to leave, she thought, *He has such a nice smile and clear hazel eyes. Even the trace of a dimple in his chin.*

And Peter, watching from the doorway, felt a nudge in his ribs and heard the lieutenant say, "Not a bad looker. I take it you've noticed!"

"That I have," answered Peter. "I think I'm going to like it here—a lot!"

29

As they sat down at the table Ann asked, "Where do you plan to begin your research, Peter?"

"I was hoping you might give me a suggestion." Peter's eyebrows raised.

"Matter-of-fact, I can. If it's not rushing you too much, Kerry plans a trip to Sapu tomorrow. There's a new believer there whom the Lord has laid on our hearts. One of us goes every so often to check in on him. Is it okay with you, Kerry, if Dr. Cameron tags along?"

"Fine with me." Looking at Peter, she

added, "We leave early. Think you can make it?"

"That's why I'm here, remember? And please, ladies, call me Peter."

"Right."

Peter grinned good-naturedly. "And now, what kind of gear will I need?"

"Your bed mat and mosquito net. We may not get back tomorrow."

"How far is Sapu?"

"About five hours hike. We'll try to head back early in the afternoon. We should cross the river by two at the latest because of the crocodiles."

"Crocodiles? Here?"

"Yes, they come in with the high tide from the open sea."

"How do you cross the river?"

Kerry and Ann exchanged glances. "We wade," said Ann. "That's the only way to get across!" At Peter's look of blank amazement, she hurried on. "Everybody does it. A native showed us the shallowest part of the river. The water at that point is only waist deep."

Peter looked from one to another. "Of course you're kidding about all this."

"No we're not! That explains why we will probably have to stay overnight. We couldn't make it there and back by two and have any ministry. That and the heat. The mid-day sun is insufferable!"

"She's right, Peter. Don't forget to wear a hat." Ann started to laugh.

"What's so funny?" queried Peter. "It all sounds rather serious to me."

"Forgive me," chuckled Ann, "but it just occurred to me that you, Peter, will be quite a novelty with your bright hair!"

The party, consisting of the missionary and Maria, as well as Solocan (who frequently accompanied the women on their trips), and the newcomer, were on their way by six a.m. After crossing the river and climbing several steep hills, they entered a wooded area with small streams and thick undergrowth. Solocan, who was keeping a close eye on Kerry, suddenly flicked a leech off her sweat-stained cheek. Kerry's hand flew up to her face in alarm. "It's gone," assured Solocan, "just caught it in time."

Kerry shuddered. "Thank you," she said fervently. Then, noting Peter's questioning look, she replied, "Leeches! I loathe them! I just can't stand the thought of those bloodthirsty creatures burying their heads in my flesh and sucking my blood! Ugh! They give me the creeps!" The men exchanged amused glances. "It's not funny," Kerry retorted. "On one hike recently, Mr. Nelson wrung blood out of his socks! If I sound paranoid," she shot an accusing look at the men, "I just can't help it. I even prayed before we left and asked the Lord to keep the leeches off of me."

Peter clapped Solocan on the back. "Looks like you're the answer to her prayer, my friend."

Solocan replied, "I am very thankful that Miss Kerry loves my people. She is willing to take the gospel to them even if it isn't easy."

It was shortly before noon when the hot and thirsty travelers reached Sapu. Donato, the new believer, welcomed them. "Thank God you have come! I have been asking Him to send you."

Inside the nipa hut, squatting on her heels in a corner, sat Dunato's wife. She was obviously frightened at the presence of the two white-skinned strangers, until her husband informed her that Kerry was the missionary who brought the story of the true God to their people. At this she relaxed and smiled, revealing teeth that had been filed and blackened.

"Many here in Sapu have been afraid because a big giant has been threatening them. Two nights ago, a voice boomed out in our house. It said, 'Give me the fingers of your wife; I want to eat'!"

"Give him your wife's fingers? You mean cut them off?" At this point Solocan interrupted for the benefit of Peter.

"My people are spirit worshippers," he explained. "They fear these spirits because they believe they bring curses and sickness and death. Often sacrifices are offered to the spirits so they will not get angry and ruin the crops. My people see these spirits and hear them speak just like Donato says."

Donato continued, "My wife and I were frightened, but I told the spirit I would not cut off my wife's fingers. When I refused, the demon shrieked at me, 'Give me the belt off your wife; I want to eat!' I answered, 'No, I am following Jesus now.' Then the spirit left, but my wife became sick with a high fever and began saying foolish things. She was like that all that night and the next day. I didn't know what to do, so I just stood beside her and prayed, 'Jesus help us!' And see, Jesus did help us. The fever left and she is in her right mind." Donato smiled at his wife. "She is well now." The woman responded with a vigorous nod of her head.

"Now I understand why the Lord laid you on our hearts to visit you," said Kerry. "How faithful He is, for even though you are the only believer here, and a new one at that, God did not fail you! Your experience demonstrates that 'the one who is greater is in you than the one who is in the world.' "

It was a joyful group that bowed in a prayer of thanksgiving. Within moments, Donato's wife trusted Christ as her Savior. It was a happy group that headed back to Glan the next day.

As for the anthropologist, Dr. Peter Cameron, he was convinced that Sapu was the place to begin his research. Donato could speak some English and, after consulting with him, Peter found him willing to help. Solocan offered to escort Peter back when he was ready to come.

"I figure I can be ready within a week," Peter decided.

That night, lying on his mat in the little hut, Peter's mind was spinning. *Things are moving very fast. I am offered the chance of a lifetime at Sapu. I should be thrilled. Why, then, this reluctance to leave Glan?*

30

The day before Peter was to leave for Sapu, he and Solocan met at the mission to finalize the details of the trip. Peter knew they must travel light, yet there were pieces of equipment that he would need. Solocan examined the load and decided that two cargadors would be sufficient to help carry it. He offered to take care of hiring them and since Bilaans do not use currency he would secure two brass gongs as payment. The gongs could be purchased from a Chinese trader for the sum of 75 pesos. Peter agreed. Solocan was about to leave when he called to Kerry, "Women are coming. I hear their bells."

Kerry hurried to the door and saw five women walking single file through the cogan grass. They were dressed in their native skirts and blouses, tiny bells stretching under their chins from ear to ear and brass anklets that clanked as they walked. They were heading straight for her house. Kerry grimaced as they spit out mouthfuls of bright red betel nut juice and wiped their mouths on their sleeves. Suddenly the women caught sight of her.

"I am happy you have come. Please enter," Kerry said in their native tongue.

They entered cautiously, all eyes focused on the white woman with blue eyes. Kerry invited them to sit down. One by one they hopped up on the bench and squatted down on their heels. This was not unusual since Bilaan huts had no furniture. Kerry sat down facing them and smiled gently. The women remained stone-faced. *Thank God Solocan is still here*, thought the missionary. *I may need him to put these women at ease.*

Solocan came at her call, followed by Peter. After talking with the women, Solocan reported that they had come from a far place to see the strange-looking foreigners. "I told them you would tell them a very good story, a true story. They are eager to hear it. Why don't you use the Sunday School chart with the colored pictures? It might help them to understand."

Kerry found the chart and opened it to a picture of Christ hanging on the cross. She plunged into the story of God's love for sinful men, a love so great that He sent His beloved Son to die in the sinner's place. The women were mystified. "God's Son? Who is God?"

Solocan interrupted. "Miss Kerry, these women have never heard of God nor Jesus nor the Bible. They have not the faintest notion what you're talking about. Start over. Talk like you would to a little child."

Kerry lifted her heart in prayer. "Oh God," she cried, "I don't even know how to begin. Help me, Father." Haltingly, prayerfully, the story began to unfold. Now the women were listening, glancing first at the chart, then at the earnest face of the missionary and back at Solocan as he interpreted. "You have come from a far place and may not be able to return here soon. I want you to remember the Name of the God Who loves you. His Name is Jesus. Will you say it so you won't forget it?"

The women looked at one another. Then, covering their mouths with their grimy hands, they began to giggle. To them the Name of Jesus was just a strange sounding word. More determined than ever, Kerry urged them on. "Jesus, it isn't hard. Say it after me. Jesus." Very faintly she heard one of them say His Name. The others turned and stared at her. Kerry prodded them on. "See, she said it. You can say it too! Try it. Jesus."

Her efforts were rewarded. She listened as five women all together said "Jesus." It was the first time they had ever spoken that Name and it seemed to the missionary that all heaven was listening.

As they were preparing to leave, Kerry invited them back. "We have a service in the chapel every Sunday." Again Solocan broke in. "They have no calendars. Every day is the same to them. Do you have a piece of string?" Kerry brought some string. Solocan proceeded to tie six knots. Pointing to the first knot, he said, "This is for today. Tomorrow you will untie this knot," pointing to the second knot. "The next day untie the next knot and do this until you get to the last knot. That's the day you come back."

The women indicated they understood but wanted to know the time. The chief's son pointed skyward to the position of the sun at ten o'clock. The women smiled and left.

Kerry watched from the door. She was not aware that Peter was standing by her until he reached down and took her hand. She looked up. His eyes held hers. He spoke, his voice suddenly gone husky. "I know why God made you a missionary! You may not realize it, little girl, but you are very, very special!"

Immediately after supper, Peter left to complete his packing. Lieutenant Castro would hold his room for him while he was in Sapu.

As the evening wore on, Kerry stepped outside for a breath of air. It was a beautiful night. The moon riding high in the sky bathed the sleeping village in it's milky light. Kerry took a deep breath, enjoying the fragrance of the dama del noche bush nearby. Seating herself on a bench, she called softly.

Pal, no longer a puppy, came bounding to her side and began to nuzzle her playfully. She cradled the shaggy head in her arms and whispered, "Pal, old boy, he thinks I'm special!" The dog responded with a moist swipe of his tongue across her soft cheeks.

Suddenly Pal stiffened. His ears shot up. A menacing growl rumbled in his throat. Kerry was startled. It was most unusual for anyone to venture out at night in this village. Peering in the distance, she saw someone approaching. She was relieved to see it was Peter.

"I see you couldn't resist being out on a night like this either," he smiled.

"I needed some of this cool air. It gets pretty stifling in there sometimes."

"So I've noticed. Care to join me for a walk?"

"I'd like that. Wait 'til I tie up the dog."

As they walked away they could hear Pal's complaining yelps. "You must get a lot of enjoyment out of that dog," Peter commented.

"He's a good companion," Kerry agreed, "especially in the evenings when there is so little to do. The villagers retire early, so it can be . . . " She was going to say "lonesome" but decided against that. "Boring," she added lamely.

Peter nodded his blond head. "I know something about that." There was a pause before he continued, his voice dropping low. "I've decided I need to make some changes."

Kerry's heart gave a leap but she didn't trust herself to answer. Then came Peter's question, blunt, honest. "I know you're very happy in your work and all, but isn't there something more you want out of life?" This time he waited for her response. It came. "I want everything the Lord has for me," Kerry replied with determination.

Her answer did not satisfy Peter but he thought it wise not to pursue the conversation further. After all, he reasoned, they had known each other only a few short weeks. Back at the house, before their final good night, Peter put his finger under Kerry's chin and tilted her face upward. Then, bending his head, he kissed her lightly on her forehead. "Just so you won't forget me," he said with one of his boyish grins.

"I promise," Kerry answered softly. "What time are you planning to leave?"

"Shortly after sunrise, if the cargadors don't foul things up. And Kerry?"

She looked up at him. "I'll be counting on your prayers."

31

Kerry's desire to teach the Bilaans to sing grew with each passing day. She had talked the matter over with Ann, who, not wishing to discourage her, commented briefly, "Sure, give it a try."

Together they carried the little pump organ into the chapel and placed it on the dirt floor. It was Sunday morning and already people were gathering, curious to see the missionaries and to hear about the One they called Jesus.

Today Ann would teach them. Kerry never failed to admire her patience and fortitude as she taught the group, seemingly undaunted by countless interruptions. The women for the most part sat huddled together talking in stage whispers and nursing their babies. The men divided their attention between the speaker and breaking up dog fights by driving the snarling creatures outside.

When the Bible lesson was over, it was Kerry's turn. As she played a few opening bars, everyone strained to listen to the magic box that made noise. "I want to teach you a song," she said. "It's a song about Jesus. Would you like to hear it?"

Big grins appeared on brown faces as her lovely voice filled the room. "What a Friend We Have in Jesus" had been translated into the Bilaan tongue. Line by line she read the lyrics, repeating them over and over.

When they seemed to have learned the words, Kerry played the melody over and over until it was time to fit words and melody together.

If she thought this would be easy, she was wrong. Kerry signaled them to join her, all the while pumping vigorously to sustain the opening note. There was a bedlam of sound! Everyone was on a different key. No one was even close to the tune of the hymn!

Kerry was appalled, unable to believe

what she was hearing. Ann was sitting in the corner trying to control a giggle. It was hot in the chapel. Beads of perspiration stood out on Kerry's brow. But she was not about to give up. Not yet.

Gritting her teeth she decided to begin again, singing and playing the tune and having them repeat after her. By this time her head was splitting, her nerves screaming. She forced a weak smile. "That will be all for now. We'll try again sometime."

These were not just idle words, for she did try again and again, doggedly, persistently, and all the while, her music-loving soul suffered. But in time, this labor of love paid off. Even Ann had to admit they were doing better than she ever thought possible. "In fact," she said, with a quiver in her voice, "I had a hard time to keep from crying when I finally recognized the words and tune of 'What a Friend We Have in Jesus'. I've got to hand it to you, Kerry," Ann spoke with enthusiasm, "I never thought you'd stick it out!"

"I came so near to giving up so many times it wasn't funny. But every time I thought about it, I felt guilty."

"Guilty? How come?"

"Because I have so much and they have

so little. Back home our church hymnal has over three hundred hymns, not to mention the scores of choruses for young people and children. Here they have one one-versed hymn!"

Ann nodded in sympathetic agreement. Kerry continued. "It's pathetic! Singing is our Christian heritage. When Christ comes into a life, He puts a song in the heart. These people need to learn how to get it out."

"I suppose that means there will be other hymns?" Ann wondered.

Kerry's face lit up. "How would you like to hear our Bilaans sing 'Take the Name of Jesus with You?' Solocan translated it a few weeks ago. Who knows? Someday we might be able to work up a choir!" At the thought she laughed outright.

"Yeah, someday. But don't hold your breath!"

32

Solocan, having just returned from Sapu, strode into the room. "Mail time! A letter for you, Miss Kerry."

Kerry extended her hand eagerly. Her cheeks turned rosy. Her eyes lit up.

"How did things go, Solocan? Is Dr. Peter all right?"

"He's okay, Miss Ann. Already he has learned a lot about our people and our ways. Maybe he will not need to stay there much longer. He has grown thin." Kerry looked up from her reading and Solocan, shrugging his shoulders, explained, "He is not used to our food."

Ann snorted. "Nothing wrong with your food: rice, fish, coconut milk, bananas. That's not exactly a reducing diet. He's probably working too hard or he might have something on his mind."

Ann's eyes twinkled mischievously. A quick glance toward Kerry found her completely engrossed in the letter. Clearing her throat, Ann asked, "How about sharing some of that with us?"

"Oh, sorry. He says, 'I am taking this opportunity to get word to you through Solocan who is returning to Glan today. I have found him and Donato to be very helpful. I never could have gotten along without them.'"

Kerry looked up and gave a salute to the chief's son who grinned broadly at the compliment. "'I am keeping well in spite of our busy days. I find I can't work much at night since the family retires early. This means early to bed for me also, so I lie there in the darkness . . .'" At that point Kerry broke off reading and, folding the letter, said faintly, "That's about it."

"Lies in the darkness, eh? Must be pretty exciting thoughts to keep him awake!" Winking at Solocan, Ann stood up. "Let me fix you a bite to eat. You must be starving."

Perched on the edge of her bed, her heart pounding, Kerry opened the letter once again and picked up from where she left off. " . . . thinking pleasant thoughts of our last evening together. I don't recall all of our conversation, for how could any man concentrate with you looking so lovely in the moonlight? I know I mentioned making some changes in my life. I will be making a quick trip to Glan on the seventh and will bring up that subject again! So please, dear girl, keep that date open. I am missing you. Hope you are missing me at least a little. Give my best to Ann." The letter was signed, "Yours ever, Peter."

Kerry sat motionless, her heart so full she thought it would burst! In her mind's eye she remembered Peter as she has seen him that night—his bright hair with highlights of gold, his hazel eyes so steadfast and clear; his patrician nose, generous mouth and chin with the slight suggestion of a dimple. "Dear Peter," she breathed, "when you come, I have something to tell you too—that I've loved you from the start!"

A light tap at her door brought Kerry back to reality. "I just heard the steamer's whistle," Ann called. "I'm on my way down to the pier. Want to tag along?"

Kerry's first impulse was to decline, then she thought better of it. After all, the arrival of the steamer was always a bright spot in their week. Who knows what they might be able to purchase from the ship's larder?

"Kerry!" a voice from behind called. Kerry turned to look into the beaming face of Jim Kendell, Peter's brother. Too astonished to speak, she blurted. "Where's Ellen? Does Peter know you're here? How long will you stay?"

"Whoa!" laughed Jim, holding up his hand as if to fend off a blow. "Let's take this one thing at a time."

"I'm so excited, so surprised to see you here. I can't wait to hear all about you and Ellen and the baby."

"Well, Ellen stayed home with the baby. She wanted to come in the worst way, but this is purely a business trip. Peter doesn't know I'm here. No telephone or telegraph connections as you know. But there is some family business that has to be settled and I need to reach Peter as soon as possible."

Back at the mission house, around the dinner table, Jim continued. "We received only one letter from him since he arrived in your island. In that letter he said how kind and helpful you had been. He did say he would be finishing his two-year stint here in the far east in a matter of four months or so and that he would stop off in Hong Kong on the way home."

"He's no doubt anxious to get acquainted with his new sister-in-law and brand new nephew," Kerry interjected.

"Yes, lots of changes have taken place since we last saw each other. But we don't anticipate a lengthy visit. He'll be wanting to get home to Valerie."

A shadow passed over Kerry's face, but Jim rambled on. "We understand there's a wedding in the offing. At least Mother seems to think so. Valerie's a lovely girl. I think Peter is a lucky guy."

Kerry sat as if carved in stone, the color slowly fading from her face. The rest of the meal was a blur as Jim's words reverberated through her tortured mind: "Eager to get home to Valerie . . . a wedding in the offing . . . Peter's a lucky guy. . . ."

To Ann's great relief, Solocan walked in. After introducing the two men, she asked if he would escort Jim to Sapu the following morning. Solocan agreed and the conversation turned to planning the trip.

When Kerry finally got to her room, she sank to her knees beside her bed, her heart thumping in her breast. *What is happening to me that I make myself believe what is not there? I was so sure he cared—his actions, his words, all the talk about making a change in his life. I was naive enough to think it involved me. All the time it was Valerie!*

Jumping to her feet she began to pace the room. Her mind raced on. She knew she could not face Peter, not now, perhaps not ever. Abruptly she stopped. "He will be here in three days," the words came out clipped, hardbitten. "He will be here. But he will not find me here when he comes!"

Kerry left the following morning for the Korondal Valley. There had been no follow-up since Ann's visit several weeks before. Ann was concerned about Kerry's leaving so abruptly, yet one look at the girl's pale face convinced her that a change would do the young missionary good. Rosa packed her bag and went along.

Sarangani Bay was a little rough that morning but Kerry welcomed the cool breeze and salt spray on her hot cheeks. She tried bravely to make small talk with Rosa, but Rosa was so miserable with fear and sea sickness that she didn't hear a word that Kerry said. Others in the small boat were sick too. It was a relief to all when the boat pulled up at the dock.

Ann had rented a small house for Kerry. It was without any conveniences, but it was situated near the bay. So, after nibbling at the lunch they had brought with them, Kerry placed her sleeping mat on the floor near an open window and lay down. She wanted so much to forget her troubled thoughts and just listen to the waves lapping the shore, but a strong face with clear hazel eyes kept intruding. With each thought of Peter the pain returned. Perhaps in time she could accept it all. In the meantime she had to believe that God makes no mistakes.

33

Peter and Jim arrived back in Glan the following morning. They had talked late into the night and now that business matters were settled, Jim was anxious to get back to Hong Kong. Both needed to shed their perspiration-soaked garments and have a cool shower before the steamer left for ports north. Jim wanted to make sure he was on that boat.

It was not until the brothers said their goodbyes that Peter turned his footsteps toward the mission. He was eager to see Kerry and to share with her what had become the compelling passion of his heart.

Peter had planned this meeting carefully. He and Kerry would go somewhere, perhaps to watch the breath-taking sunset. He was planning to tell her something she already knew. There was only one small cloud on the horizon—her complete dedication to her missionary call. Peter frowned slightly as he tried to remember the verse he had heard her quote, something about putting your hand to the plow and not looking back. But the fact remained that God had brought them together in this far-away land and filled his heart with a consuming love for her.

Time and again Peter reassured himself that her call need not be a problem. After all, he was a missionary at heart too. He had dedicated his life to Christ in high school during a missionary conference at the local church. Admittedly his life had taken a slightly different direction, but he, Peter, wanted God's will for His life too.

Peter's pace quickened as he approached the missionary residence. In two bounds, he was standing inside the open door. "Anybody home?" he called, his pulse accelerating with excitement.

Ann greeted him warmly. "Peter! We

weren't expecting you so soon, but I'm glad you've come."

"Jim was anxious to get home, so I put him on the boat this morning," Peter explained.

"Well, you're just in time for a bite of lunch. You two must have left Sapu early."

"Trying to beat the heat," Peter added. "Jim insisted on catching that steamer." Sniffing the air, Peter asked, "Is that real coffee I'm smelling?"

"With home-made biscuits and jelly! How does that grab you?"

"Couldn't be better!" Pulling back the chair he sat down. Ann poured him a steaming cup of coffee. "Where is the beauteous Irish maiden? Doesn't she believe in eating lunch?"

Ann swallowed hard. That was the question she had been dreading. "Uh, she's not here, Peter. She's spending the week in the Korondal Valley."

Peter looked up at Ann, his eyes wide and questioning. Ann shrugged helplessly. "She decided to follow up on my visit. It's been a while."

Peter, obviously shaken, asked, "Was this something she had planned earlier?"

"No, it was a last-minute decision. I

reminded her that she would miss your visit but she felt this was important." Ann could have bitten her tongue at her choice of words.

Peter flushed to the roots of his hair. "So she did get my letter." His voice was scarcely audible.

"Oh yes. We were all glad to get a word from you."

Peter had one more question. Trying desperately to control his voice, he turned to Ann. "Did she leave any message?"

Ann shook her head. "She left in such a hurry," she said lamely. "I'm not even sure where in the valley she is. She mentioned visiting Tupi and the new settlement, Marbel. I'm sorry, Peter."

Ann's motherly heart went out to the young man. He looked so crushed, so bewildered. Ann waved limply as he reached the door.

"Now what was that all about?" Ann wondered aloud. "For a man engaged to this Valerie, he sure seemed upset when Kerry wasn't here!" Throwing her hands in the air and rolling her eyes heavenward, she muttered, "Men! I give up!"

The walk back to the barracks was just a blur for Peter. Kerry's deliberate departure angered him. But greater than the anger was the conviction that he would never stop loving her.

"I'm going to keep hoping, little girl," he said piteously. "Oh Kerry! Oh God!" It was a cry of despair for Peter was powerless to do anything about it.

34

Kerry pulled herself onto the rickety bus heading for Marbel. Although neither she nor Ann had ever been there, she felt sure the Visayans, noted for their hospitality, would offer her and Rosa lodging.

The six-hour trip was tortuous, with the over-crowded bus lurching and plunging over the badly rutted road. At one point, the bus gently tipped over and came to rest in the ditch. The passengers riding on the roof merely stepped off. The closeness of perspiring bodies, the suffocating heat, the erratic movement of the bus, compounded by the squealing of several frightened pigs, left Kerry little room to nurse her heartache. And added to the physical discomfort was the very real concern for survival!

Finally the nightmare was over. Her body stiff and sore, Kerry gingerly followed the other passengers off the bus. Behind her, Rosa stumbled out. They walked over to a large store-like structure. As far as Kerry could see, the tiny settlement was completely barren of trees and vegetation. The houses appeared small, raised up on stilts, laid out in neat rows along the dusty road.

As Kerry and Rosa stood in the heat, wondering what to do next, a young boy appeared. He spoke in broken English. "I'll ask can you stay with us?" And he was off, running as fast as his spindly legs would carry him. In no time he was back, nodding his head vigorously and smiling. He picked up Kerry's suitcase and bolted off again. Both women hurried after him, glad for a chance to stretch their legs.

The boy stopped before a nipa hut which looked exactly like all the others. An old woman stood in the doorway watching them. No sooner had Kerry mounted the bamboo ladder than she heard a quavering voice. "You are a Bible woman?"

"Why yes," responded Kerry. Tears spilled down the woman's wrinkled cheeks.

"We have been waiting for someone to teach us the Word of God. At last you have come!"

What if she had not come, Kerry wondered. *How much longer would they have waited?* With a smile Kerry promised they would have a Bible study that very night.

Two younger women appeared and welcomed the visitors warmly. Kerry and Rosa were conducted to their sleeping quarters—a wooden bed made of solid planks. There was very little furniture in the house, but their hostess did have some bowls and glasses. True to Filipino style, they were soon offered a refreshing drink of calamunsi juice. Kerry drained the glass. Her hostess refilled it and she drank that too.

Night descended, and with it came rain, a veritable downpour. Word had gotten around about the meeting and in spite of the weather the settlers began arriving, each one carrying a flare to light his way. Soon the room was filled with men and women squatting on their heels, broad smiles wreathing their weather-beaten faces. Kerry kept her message simple.

At the close of the meeting someone asked, "Can we do this again tomorrow night?" Kerry agreed. The second night someone asked. "Can you send us someone to live with us and be our pastor? We will build him a house and build a meeting place."

Kerry assured them that she would remember their request.

Three kilometers north of Dadiangas was another small community. Ann had visited it during her brief stay in the valley. Since Kerry would pass very near there on her way back, she decided to stop by. Rosa went on to Dadiangas.

Kerry's arrival made quite a stir and soon children came running from every quarter, clapping their hands when they saw her. Several adults gathered around too. The Bible story prompted many questions. This was delaying her journey to Dadiangas, but they were so hungry for spiritual things that she put her fears of the road behind her and concentrated on the moment. When Kerry finally said she had to leave, they insisted she stay overnight. The trail was dangerous after dark, they cautioned. Snakes and black-widow spiders lurked in the tall grass. She would be overtaken by darkness long before she reached Dadiangas. However, remembering Rosa's fear of being alone, Kerry responded that she would have to be on her way.

She was not far down the trail when the sky began to darken. Here, so near the equator, there is no twilight—the curtain of night drops swiftly. Within a matter of minutes she found herself in deep darkness. There were no homes, no people, not even a star overhead—just a vast sea of blackness. Caution demanded that she step carefully as the slender beam of her flashlight pointed out the trail.

The stillness was suddenly broken by noises ahead. Kerry decided it was the bawling of carabaos. She had heard of the massive wild buffalo with their murderous horns. Swinging her flashlight in a wide circle, she located the herd heading her way. Kerry trained the light on their glittering eyes. Frightened or blinded, she didn't know which, the animals veered off and disappeared into the night.

It was a very tired and relieved Kerry who finally emerged from the dark, grassy trail to feel the sands of Dadiangas under her feet. In no time she was knocking at the guest house door, calling Rosa's name. She heard the bolt slide back. A tall shadow emerged against the dim light. It was Solocan.

"Miss Kerry," he exclaimed, "how did you get here?"

"Like everybody else gets here," she answered curtly. "I hiked!"

Solocan shook his head in stern disapproval. "That was a very risky thing to do."

Kerry bristled. "Look here, Solocan, I'm not trying to live dangerously. I know it's foolish to take unnecessary risks, but sometimes it can't be avoided. Now, if you don't mind, I'd like to come in."

Solocan stepped aside as Kerry brushed past him. She turned to face him. "I'm sorry I spoke that way. It was pretty awful out there. I'm tired." She held out her hands appealingly. Solocan nodded. "I guess I didn't sound very sympathetic either. I was just thinking of the danger. Thank God you did make it safely."

"I am grateful. Now how does it happen that you're here?" questioned Kerry.

"Miss Ann suggested I come in case you needed my help."

"I sure could have used it tonight," Kerry responded wearily. Then, hoping for news of Peter, she asked, "Everything all right in

Glan?" It was hard to keep the urgency out of her voice.

Solocan lowered his eyes before the intensity of her look. "Things are as usual, except for Dr. Peter. He came to Glan the day you left and surprised us with the announcement that he would be going back to the States soon." He paused, waiting for her reaction. When there was none, he finished lamely, "Outside of that, nothing new."

Kerry forced a fleeting smile. "I hope his stay in Sapu has been profitable. I know ours was here. I have accomplished what I set out to do in more ways than one."

Solocan's eyes rested on her. "Does that mean you are ready to return to Glan?" he asked.

"I am ready. Unless you have other plans, we can go home tomorrow."

35

Those two inviting drinks of calamunsi juice in Marbel were now taking their toll. At first Kerry attributed her totally wretched state to the situation with Peter. Surely life would never be the same. She could never love another, not ever! Most frightening of all was her seeming inability to snap out of this depression. Languishing in the doldrums was a new experience for this high-spirited young woman.

Ann, hesitant to pry, remained a concerned onlooker. Once or twice she tried to tactfully mention Peter, hoping that Kerry would open up, but these advances only met with silence.

"What is it Kerry? What's wrong?" Ann noticed Kerry doubled over in pain.

"I'm not sure, but it's awful." Kerry clutched her abdomen.

"How long have you been feeling like this?"

"I've had a few rumblings inside this past week, but today is much worse."

"Sounds to me like you have picked up some amoeba, or . . . "

"Or what?"

"I don't want to frighten you, but perhaps it could be appendicitis. Whatever it is, it's nothing to fool around with. You need medical help."

"And where will I get that here?"

"You can't get it here. You'll have to go somewhere where you can get it. There's is a pretty good hospital in Zamboanga City."

"But that's three or four days from here!"

"I know. We can't waste any time. You really should have this cared for immediately."

Kerry, too ill to offer further resistance, was soon headed for Zamboanga City.

Meanwhile, Peter was trying to wind down his work in Sapu. He had accomplished more than he ever dreamed possible in his short time there, due to the able help of Sabid and Solocan. By the end of the month, just a week away, he would be on his way. It wouldn't be easy to leave his friends in Sapu, especially Sabid. He had come to love him like a brother.

Peter's arrival in Glan was without fanfare. He had planned it that way, not knowing if Kerry would be there or not. Hearing that she had gone to Zamboanga City, he felt somewhat relieved. At least he would not have to face her. The very thought of her sent spasms of pain through his heart. How could he endure seeing her, being in the same room with her, without taking her in his arms and pleading his case?

But no. She had deliberately left town to avoid him. He must accept her decision for the time being. The meeting that he had been agonizing over was not to be. At least he must find out from Ann how she was getting along. Ann would know.

Ann, as always, was happy to see him. After the greetings were over, she read Kerry's letter to Peter. Her suspicions were correct: it was amoebic dysentery, plus general anemia. The doctor had ordered complete bed rest and the medication seemed to be working. Kerry was feeling better and hoping it wouldn't be long before she would be permitted to return to Glan. "As soon as the doctor gives the green light," she wrote, "I'll be on the first boat back."

"She's starting to sound like the old Kerry," quipped Ann, "but she had me worried for a while."

Peter turned away and walked over to the window. "I'm glad to hear she's better," he said stoically. "When you see her, tell her I said goodbye."

36

Both Jim and Ellen were looking forward to Peter's visit. Ellen especially was excited, for this was the first member of Jim's family that she would meet. "Does Peter look like you?" she asked Jim. "Do you think he will like me?"

"Sweetheart," Jim's strong arms drew her close, "that's a dumb question. How can he not help liking my gorgeous wife and beautiful baby? Of course he will."

Ellen wrinkled her nose. "I'm not at all gorgeous, dearest, but if you think so, that's all that matters to me."

At the pier, Jim noticed Peter first and

began waving. "That's him," he pointed, "the fellow with the blond hair."

Peter saw them. Cupping his hand around his mouth, he shouted something that was lost in the din of the waterfront. A moment later he was off the gangplank and the brothers were giving each other a big bear hug. Meanwhile Ellen, holding Davey, stood quietly by. Jim turned and put his arm around her. "My gifts from God—Ellen and Davey!"

Peter gave Ellen a long look before bending his head and planting a kiss on her cheek. "You're as lovely as Jim said you were," he said simply. "Thank you for making my brother a very happy man." Then, turning to the wriggling youngster in Ellen's arms, he squeezed the chubby legs that had escaped the blanket.

"So this is Davey!" The baby chortled his delight and held out his arms. Peter took him from Ellen. "Little nephew," he whispered, "you and I are going to be great friends." Still holding him close, Peter followed Jim and Ellen to their car.

"How is my good friend Kerry?" Ellen inquired as they sat down to apple pie and coffee.

The question twisted like a knife in Peter's heart. He lowered his fork and struggled to appear casual. "She was ill when I left. Actually, she was hospitalized."

"Oh no!" broke in Ellen.

"But she's coming along all right and hopes to get back to work soon."

"What was the problem?"

"Some sort of intestinal infection, I understand. I don't know any details."

"Poor Kerry. I can't imagine her sick. She was always so healthy. I guess you know we were cabinmates on the trip over?"

Peter nodded assent. "I've heard you two are very good friends." He wished fervently that the subject would change, but Ellen rambled on.

"She's one of my best friends, although I knew her for only a few short weeks. We try to keep in touch, which reminds me she owes me a letter. I wrote a few weeks ago but I suppose she has been too busy or sick to write."

"She always seems to be busy," Peter added. Then, abruptly changing the subject, he turned to his brother. "Jim, old boy, it seems unreal, sitting here with you and your family in your cozy apartment and seeing how happy you are here." With a sweep of his hand that included Ellen and Davey, he added, "It seems you've got everything. I can't tell you how happy I am for you."

Jim smiled. "You know what the Good Book says, 'He who finds a wife finds what is good and receives favor from the Lord!' You'll know what I'm talking about after you and Valerie tie the knot."

A startled look passed over Peter's face. "Oh, yes. I guess the last word you had was that Val and I were pretty serious. But that's finished now. It has been over about two years."

Jim was visibly shocked. "Finished? How come?"

"By mutual consent. I knew I would be gone on my assignment. Two years seemed a long time to Val. In case you've forgotten, she's a popular young lady. I didn't think it was fair to tie her down. She agreed."

"Oh, I'm sorry, Peter."

"It's all right, Jim. We're still good friends, but both of us know that God never intended us for one another. I sure know that now more than ever." His voice trailed off.

Ellen broke in. "Well, that is news! In my letter to Kerry . . . oh-h-h Davey!" Everyone turned just in time to see the baby's milk cascading down Peter's pant leg. "Great, just great! He hasn't done that in a long time," Jim apologized. "He would have to show off now!"

"Oh, it's nothing a dry cleaner can't fix. You do have dry cleaners in Hong Kong?"

"The best! I'll take your trousers down there as soon as you change."

"Can I finish my pie first?" Peter insisted. "You forget I haven't had pie for two years."

37

Kerry, healthy young specimen that she was, recovered quickly. Once back in Glan she plunged wholeheartedly into her work. Among those who came to her Friday night Bible study was a teenager named Mina Duno, and her younger sister, Rana. They were from a Muslim/pagan background but were very interested in the gospel. They never missed a class.

One evening, Kerry noticed that Mina came alone. Something must be wrong. The sisters always came together. Besides, it was against the custom for a female to travel alone at night.

"You are alone tonight?" Kerry asked Mina. "Where is Rana?"

Pointing to the door, Mina whispered, "She's out there." Kerry was mystified. "Why is she outside? Why didn't she come in?"

"There was an accident."

"What happened?" Before Mina could answer, Kerry was at the door. She could barely see the little girl in the darkness, rocking back and forth, trying to stifle her sobs. Kerry dropped to her knees beside her. She could see a badly swollen foot. Cradling the injured foot in her hands, she asked, "A snake?"

"No, mum," Mina answered, "it was a poisonous centipede. We didn't have enough oil in the flares. She stepped on it."

Kerry's heart went out to the suffering child. Turning to Mina, she demanded, "Why didn't you tell me? It was cruel to leave her here all alone."

Mina flinched. "She asked me not to tell you. She was afraid you would stop the Bible study. She begged me to just leave her and go in. Then I could tell her what you said."

Kerry's arm went around the girls. "I'll get something to make your foot better."

And to Mina, "I'm sorry. I didn't understand. Stay with her. I'll be right back."

Kerry returned with a basin of water, medication and bandages. Tenderly she bathed the foot and put on a soft bandage. The tears had stopped by now. Kerry gave the girls a hug and watched as they melted into the darkness.

Kerry's eyes moistened at the thought of this little girl who was so hungry to learn about Jesus that she willingly bore such pain. How thankful Kerry was to be here sharing the good news!

Intent upon her thoughts, she failed to notice that Solocan had joined her. "You really do love my people," he said, impulsively gripping her by the shoulders. Startled, Kerry turned. Solocan released her, bowed and walked away.

"Good night, Solocan," she called after him. "Thanks for taking over for me at the close." She saw him turn and wave, never guessing the tumult that was in his heart.

Solocan spent a sleepless night. No longer could he deny the feeling he had for Kerry. That she liked him, there was no doubt. Her appreciation for his help was sincere. And she trusted him. Difficult as it was going to be, he would not presume upon her frank and open friendship. But she was unattached. She loved his people. And she was lonely. "Oh God," he prayed, "how long will I be able to keep her from knowing?"

Solocan's behavior disturbed Kerry, but she finally concluded that he intended no disrespect. It had been a thoughtless gesture. She was sure it would not be repeated.

"Time is passing, Solocan," Kerry reminded him. "If we're going to get in that trip to Baliton, we'd better get going." Actually she had been dreading the trip and had been putting it off despite the urging of Solocan.

The trail was steep and rough, she knew, far worse than anything they had tackled yet. That meant it was pretty bad. But she could not forget that there were people in Baliton who needed to hear about God's gift of eternal life in Christ Jesus. She could procrastinate no longer. They would leave the following morning.

Solocan was solicitous of Kerry on the trail, but she thought nothing of it. He had always helped her when the going was rough and today the feel of his strong hand under her elbow was comforting. At one point where the trail seemed to go straight up, Solocan took her hand and, flinging her arm across his shoulder, half pulled, half carried her. Both were panting for breath, straining every muscle. *How strong and considerate,* Kerry thought to herself. *Could this be the same man that a few years ago threatened my life?*

Eventually they reached the top of the mountain. Solocan let go of her hand and leaned against a giant tree. "I'm sorry I am such a burden," Kerry apologized. "I'm not very good at . . . . " But Solocan cut her off. "You are never a burden, Miss Kerry. You are a plucky little lady to tackle this trip. It gives me joy to be of service." His eyes found hers. Had they revealed more than he intended?

Kerry looked down. "Thank you. I'd have never been able to negotiate this trail without you!"

Solocan turned to Rosa. "Let's get out the lunch. We need a break. Besides, I'm starved!" They were soon munching rice and dried fish, with a banana for dessert. *Everything seems to be perfectly normal,* Kerry thought to herself. *But why do I feel so uncomfortable?*

It was late in the afternoon before the exhausted hikers stumbled into Baliton. Solocan escorted the women to the home of the school teacher and then headed to a relative's house. There would be no meeting that night.

Soon supper was ready—corned beef, which Kerry had brought along, plus eggs and rice and the ever-present banana supplied by the hostess. The conversation around the table was punctuated by Rosa's yawns. The hostess suggested that the women should retire early. It had been a long day.

After making sure that the mosquito net was tucked securely around her, Kerry stretched out on her sleeping mat on the floor. Within moments she was asleep. The moonlight, sifting through the coconut palms outside the open window, played upon her features. A slight frown furrowed her forehead. As was so often the case lately, she was dreaming of Peter. They were strolling beside the pier at sunset. But suddenly, the sun was gone. Darkness fell. Searching for an explanation, she looked up at Peter. Only it was no longer Peter—it was Solocan!

Kerry sat upright on her mat, her heart pounding. The night was warm, but shivers went up and down her spine. Slowly the room came into focus. She could identify Rosa's net. And yes, the dim form of the sleeping girl. *Oh God, it was just a dream. I'm thankful it was just a dream.*

38

The people of Baliton proved to be very receptive to the gospel. Solocan secured permission to use the town plaza for the nightly open-air meetings. Children's meetings were held during the day. Since the teacher's house was elevated on stilts, it provided a large shaded area underneath and youngsters thronged there by the dozens. They were enthralled by the colorful stories. Kerry decided to extend their stay to three days. Even then it was hard to leave.

The trip back to Glan was exhausting. Kerry made up her mind to be more independent, not to depend so much on Solocan. She tried to keep the conversation flowing as they walked, but that was not so easy when one was out of breath. Each lapse into silence made her nervous. Her dream still haunted her. She could not help but be aware of Solocan's nearness—his muscular physique and his thoughtful concern for her. She chattered on and on.

"Relax, Miss Kerry. Save your breath for the trail," Solocan advised.

Kerry's foot caught in the roots of a tree. She stumbled, but Solocan caught her and held her until she regained her footing. "Thanks," Kerry muttered. "Guess I was not watching."

To the relief of all, the trip finally ended. They were back in Glan.

Inside the mission house, Ann scrutinized Kerry. "You look terrible! Hard trip?"

"Yes," groaned Kerry, slumping into a chair, "Oh my aching bones!" Then brightening, "But it was worth it. The people in Baliton were so eager to hear. Anything exciting happen here?" Kerry wanted to know.

A hint of a smile moved over Ann's lips. "You might say so. You had a visitor while you were gone."

"A visitor? Who?"

"Bob Wilson. He had a favor to ask of you."

Kerry was puzzled, "What on earth could it be?"

"He'll tell you when he returns. He left on the steamer for Davao when he learned you weren't here. Said he would be back in a couple of days."

"Did he tell you what this favor was?"

"Yes, but I think he wants to ask you himself. The only reason I mentioned it to you was that he wants to make sure you are here when he returns. I told him I thought you'd be glad to stay home for a few days after that trip to Baliton."

"You won't give me even a little hint?"

"No. He made it quite plain that he wants to explain it all to you when he comes."

"You make it sound so mysterious." The young missionary was very tired.

"Nothing mysterious about it," laughed Ann. "You may even find it exciting."

Kerry shrugged her shoulders and, pulling herself out of the chair, headed for her room. "The only thing that excites me right now is a shower, some of your good cooking and bed."

Kerry slept late the next morning and, except for sore muscles, was none the worse for the stresses of the previous days.

But why am I thinking of Solocan? Kerry shook her head as if to brush away her thoughts. *You'd better quit right now!*

But she was young and lonely and longed for the kind of relationship she thought she had had with Peter. Peter! A sadness crept across her face. *No use thinking of the past and what can never be. This is today and from this moment on I will control my thoughts.*

Some things, however, are easier said than done.

"I see you haven't suffered any ill effects from the journey." Kerry turned to face Solocan. She hadn't noticed him come in. She was busy trying to tone down the youthful bedlam of the Friday night gathering.

"Oh, I survived," she quipped, "but it wasn't easy." Both laughed, recalling her lack of skill at mountain climbing. "It was rough on you, Miss Kerry, but . . . "

"Let me guess," she interrupted, wagging a finger at him. "After all Christ has done for us this isn't too much to do for Him."

"You're right!" he grinned. "You can quote me there. And Miss Kerry . . . "

"Yes?"

"I have a feeling you'd do it all over again."

"Not tomorrow," she answered groaning. "Right now we have another job to do. Let's get at it."

It was a good meeting—informal, lively, spontaneous. It did Kerry's heart good to see how these once painfully shy youngsters had come out of their shell, asking and answering questions and sharing their experiences. Solocan was developing into a truly gifted leader. With a little Bible training . . . . She stopped short. *Watch out old girl. There you go again!*

The meeting ended and the young people were filing out. Kerry made sure she had a few words with each one. She especially wanted to talk to Julio, a newcomer, but Solocan had him to one side. She watched them from the door.

She noticed the compassionate look on Solocan's face and the attention of Julio riveted on the book Solocan held in his hand. Several minutes passed. Still she watched, a conviction growing in her soul. Now they were kneeling. Solocan's arm went around the younger man's shoulders.

This affection she felt for the chief's son?

Was he not a brother in Christ? Were they not both concerned about reaching the lost? Did they not share the same vision? "Oh, God," Kerry prayed, "we are both members of the family of God and You have commanded us to love one another. Solocan is especially dear to me because You gave me the privilege of leading him to you."

As the mists of confusion lifted, Kerry breathed a sigh of relief. Her struggle over Solocan was settled. Her mind was at peace, her heart at rest. She would love him as a brother in Christ—nothing more, nothing less.

"Julio just accepted Christ as His Savior. He is one of us now," announced a beaming Solocan.

Before Kerry found her voice, Julio added, "Mum, you know I have been feeling that we here in Glan were forgotten." He struggled to explain. "Is it not true that we have very little here? No roads, no schools, no hospital? Civilization has passed us by. But God did not forget us. He sent you here to tell us the way of salvation."

The words went like an arrow to Kerry's heart.

"You speak the truth, Julio. God did not

forget you. He thought of you when he hung on Calvary's cross. That's why He was there—to pay our debt of sin. He loved us then and He loves us now."

Lifting luminous eyes to Solocan, Kerry added, "My brother here, and I, welcome you into the family of God!"

39

Kerry stared at Bob Wilson. "You can't be serious!" she exclaimed.

Bob, knowing that the task given to him would not be easy, spoke quietly and firmly. "I'm sorry I have to break it to you like this. I know it is a bolt out of the blue, but the situation is critical. If there was any other option, the board would have suggested it." His voice took on a tone of finality, "I'm sorry."

Kerry wheeled and walked over to the window, her back to Bob. Suddenly she faced him, flushed and angry. "Why me?" she demanded.

"I thought I explained that," Bob answered patiently. "You are next in line for furlough."

Kerry opened her mouth to protest, but Bob silenced her with an upraised hand. "Yes, I know, Marj and I have been here longer. Our furlough was due six months ago. But since I am acting field chairman, you must realize that I can't leave until Doug gets back. It looks as if that will be several weeks yet. Amy can't wait."

For the first time Kerry felt compassion for the sick missionary. Somewhat calmer, she ventured to ask, "You haven't mentioned what Amy's trouble is."

"Overwork has brought on what appears to be a nervous breakdown. She can't eat. She can't sleep. She is despondent and cries most of the time. The doctor insists she return to the States and get medical attention. We can't let her go alone. In her present state of mind it just isn't safe. Somebody must go with her."

Kerry was sympathetic but the burden for the work among the tribespeople overwhelmed her.

"But there is so much yet to do here," she insisted.

"Granted. But the work here will not go

uncared for. You know that as well as I do. Ann and Solocan will make a great team. He certainly has proven himself to be able and willing. They will do fine."

"So it's settled?" Kerry questioned once again.

"I'm afraid so." Then, hoping to cheer her up, Bob continued, "But it's not all bad. Look on the bright side. Why, with your gifts you'll be kept busy speaking in the churches. Think of the opportunities you'll have to present the needs of these tribespeople back home. Get them to praying, Kerry. God knows we need it. Don't you see? You'll be serving the cause of missions there too."

Bob's persuasive powers were taking effect, but Kerry would not give in easily. "Well, it isn't what I would have chosen, but if this is the decision of the board, I will comply." There was a brief silence.

"We never know what's around the next bend in the road, do we? I . . . I guess God wants us to trust Him even when we can't understand."

Bob heaved a sigh of relief. "Spoken like a real trooper, my girl. You've made the right decision. God will bless you for it. Now," he took a deep breath, "here's the million dollar question: how soon can you be ready?"

It was like a bad dream, being plucked away so unceremoniously with little time for preparation. As the night dragged on, Kerry kept reminding herself that it was Amy who must be considered. That faithful missionary had worn herself out serving others. Now it was Kerry's turn to help her. The words of Jesus kept buzzing in her mind, "Whatever you did for one of the least of these brothers of mine, you did for me."

All right, Lord. I accept this and I will do it, not grudgingly, but willingly, as unto You.

"You're what?" Solocan's black eyes flashed. "You're leaving us? You're leaving the work here to . . . to babysit a missionary?"

Solocan put his hand over his eyes. "I'm sorry, I was wrong to speak to you like that. I know you well enough to know you are suffering at the thought of leaving the work here. It's just that I'm not ready for this."

"Neither am I. But Amy is critically ill and must return to the States immediately. My superiors feel it is not wise to send her alone."

"So you're elected!" The edge crept back into his voice. Solocan crossed his arms. "And there's no one else in the whole mission to handle this but you?"

Kerry shrugged wearily. "They make the decisions. They do what they feel is best for all."

"Well, it's not best for us, for the work here!" Kerry could only nod in agreement. "When will you leave?"

"Next week, when the steamer returns from Davao."

"That soon?" Then as if speaking to himself, "In just one week you will be gone."

Kerry nodded as Solocan took a deep breath and expelled it slowly. Solocan was not usually given to panic, but his voice was shaky. "I guess there's nothing we can do. When the chief gives an order...." His voice trailed off. For a few tense moments both struggled for composure.

Moved by Kerry's tears, he said gently, "Don't cry, Miss Kerry." Placing a finger under her chin, he tilted her face upward. "Hey, remember me? I'm the guy that had to haul you over the mountain!" Then more seriously, "While you're away, dear friend," he paused and with an effort cleared his throat, "I'll do my best to spread the message you brought to us."

Impulsively, Kerry reached for his hand. Bowing her head she cradled it between her two hands. "Dear, dear brother and special friend!"

Briefly she felt his free hand rest lightly on her head. Then releasing himself from her grasp, he strode out of the room. There was never a backward glance.

Kerry watched, wondering at his swift departure. There was a huge lump in her throat. *I thought the worst was over when I said goodbye to my family in Albany. But saying goodbye to my spiritual family here is just as hard.*

It would have been even harder had she known then that in this life she would never see Solocan Napila again.

40

Solocan was not among those who gathered at the pier to say goodbye. Kerry knew it was not easy on Ann either to see her go. Putting her arms around her, she whispered, "Thank you, Ann, for all you have taught me. I'll be a better missionary for it."

Ann hugged her back. "You've been a brick, Kerry. You've done a good job. Hurry back!"

From the rail, Kerry searched the crowd for Solocan. He was nowhere to be found. Finally, the little village that had been home for over four years slowly faded in the distance. Still Kerry stood at the rail. Would she ever return? Why did God permit her to be routed out? Was she not needed now more than ever? Could Ann handle everything? The outreach? The services in town? She couldn't possibly do it even with Solocan's help. The work of the Lord among the Bilaans would surely suffer.

Again the Holy Spirit reminded her of the words of Jesus, " . . . on this rock I will build my church, and the gates of Hades shall not overcome it" (Matthew 16:18). Tension began to drain from her body. *Thank You, dear Lord,* she prayed, *for reminding me that I am not indispensable! With me or without me, Your work will go on.*

Bob Wilson and Amy were waiting for Kerry in Manila. Bob had made arrangements to fly the missionaries home since Amy might not be able to endure rough ocean travel. Kerry was relieved. Twenty-one days on board ship with a sick missionary was not a pleasant prospect. Her only disappointment lay in the fact that the plane would by-pass Hong Kong. She had long ago made up her mind that enroute home she would visit Ellen. It would be great renewing their friendship, not to mention the fact that Ellen's husband was

Peter's brother. It was a bitter pill for Kerry to swallow.

Amy bore up well during the flight. Her parents were at the airport to meet them. They welcomed Amy lovingly, then turned to Kerry. "Thank you for accompanying Amy home. Be our guest for a few days. There's a lot to see around Los Angeles," they offered. "We'll be happy to show you the sights." But Kerry was chomping at the bit to get home to her own family.

"Thank you, that's very kind of you, but I'm taking the first plane east. Albany, here I come!"

There was Dad, slightly heavier, with a little more gray at the temples. He was at the head of the line, his arms extended. Kerry rushed into his strong arms. Soon hugs and kisses were flying thick and fast until George interrupted. "Okay, tribe, we can finish this at home after Kerry gets one of Sue's good meals under her belt." Holding Kerry at arms length, he added, "You look as if you could use a few!"

It was clear to the McCormicks that subtle changes had taken place in Kerry. Not only was she older, but she was less vivacious. A certain sadness settled on her face when she was not entertaining them with one story or another. Her father's keen eyes were often on his beloved daughter, wondering what had changed her from an enthusiastic youngster when she left them to the thoughtful subdued woman she had become.

Then came Solocan's first letter. Kerry flushed with pleasure.

> Dear Miss Kerry:
> I have great news for you! Just a few days after you left us, the Lord did something special to cheer our sad hearts. You remember Sabid from Balut? I know you do. He has been witnessing to his people using the Sunday School charts you gave him. Imagine our surprise to see five vintas tie up at the wharf and thirty men enter the chapel. This was last Sunday. And this is how they introduced themselves. 'Sabid has been telling us about Jesus, the true God Who died for our sins. We have accepted this Jesus and Sabid sent us to you to be baptized!'
> We examined these men to see if they really understood the gospel. Well, Sabid had done a good job. They un-

derstood, so we baptized them. How we wish you could have been here!

Well, now they are asking for a preacher because Sabid has told them all he knows. They promise to build a house for the pastor and also a chapel. I am leaving today for Balut and will stay there for a while. Sabid will come to Glan to help Miss Ann and to learn more from her. I hope you are having a good visit with your family, but don't forget what Jesus said, 'The harvest is plentiful but the workers are few!'

Yours for lost souls,
Solocan Napila

Kerry was ecstatic. Clasping the letter to her heart she said softly, "Dear Solocan."

"This Solocan person means a lot to you?" Mr. McCormick asked.

"Yes, Daddy," Kerry admitted, "but not in the way you may be thinking. Solocan is," she was searching for words, " 'a trophy of God's grace.' He means a lot to me because I had the privilege of leading him to Christ."

"Why that's wonderful!" broke in Sue. "How did that happen?"

"I hope you're ready for this." With that,

Kerry launched into the story of how God delivered Solocan from the power of demons and cleansed his heart.

"Whew!" Tracy exhaled slowly. "How come you never mentioned that in your letters?"

"I did tell you about Solocan," responded Kerry. "I just left out a few of the details."

41

Bob Wilson's prophecy that Kerry would be kept busy speaking in churches came true. Kerry's presentation of the missionary challenge was stirring and forceful. Invitations continued to pour in. Every time she faced an audience the words of Bob Wilson reverberated in her heart: "Get them praying. God knows we need it!" Every message was geared to that theme.

Kerry had just completed a three-month tour. She was exhausted. All she wanted to do was to go home and rest. So it was understandable that she asked to be excused from a conference that was slated to begin immediately after the regular tour.

"I'm awfully tired," she pleaded. "Ask one of the other missionaries." But it seemed there was no one else to go.

"Where is this church located?" Kerry wanted to know.

"In Pennsylvania, not far from Scranton."

"How come they waited so long to invite a speaker?"

"The speaker they booked had to cancel at the last minute for health reasons. The pastor is in a jam and called for help." Kerry stared at the district superintendent. "It's a fine missionary-minded church," he added. "You'll have a good time there. Now, about your transportation—I'm free this afternoon. I'll drive you there."

Several hours later Kerry entered the sanctuary of the church. Her glance caught a lone figure adjusting the slide projector in the center aisle.

That hair! That lean muscular form! She clapped her hand over her mouth to stifle a sob that begged to escape. Peter turned and held out his arms.

"Peter!" For a moment, the world and everything in it was forgotten. Peter held her in a strong embrace as if to never let her go.

Suddenly Kerry remembered and pushed away. "Valerie?" It was just a whispered word.

Peter reached for her. "Dearest," his voice was strained. "There is no Valerie. There has never been anyone else, my darling, but you!"

"I don't understand." But Peter's eager lips silenced her questions. "Kerry, you do love me? Kerry, oh Kerry, why did you run away?"

A rosy flush spread up her cheeks. "Because I heard you were going to marry Valerie!"

"It's you I love, Kerry. I loved you back in Glan and my love for you has grown with each passing day. Don't make me wait any longer. Say you will marry me!"

Lifting her face to his, Kerry whispered, "I thought you'd never ask!"

A discreet cough in the background interrupted. "Dr. Jerome, our missionary had arrived," Peter blurted.

The pastor's eyes were twinkling. "It appears you have met before!"

"In the Philippines," Peter explained. "Kerry, uh, Miss McCormick, was a great help in getting me started in my work there."

The pastor extended his hand. "I'm delighted you're here. Mr. Cameron suggested your name as a possible speaker for our conference."

Kerry looked at Peter. "Then you were expecting me?"

"Yes, I answered the phone when the district superintendent called to say the replacement was a certain Miss McCormick."

"And his recommendation was most enthusiastic!" The pastor smiled broadly. Dr. Jerome had counselled many couples who were in love and recognized the symptoms. "I'll leave you two to plan tonight's meeting."

"It sounds like you're the assistant pastor here. How did that happen, Peter?" Kerry asked.

Peter's eyes had a far away look. "Well, while I was in the Philippines, I observed a gallant young woman pouring out her life for neglected people. I looked around and saw the need first hand. So I promised the Lord that as soon as I got home I would go to seminary. When I graduated, I was assigned to help Dr. Jerome here."

"And after this?"

Peter caught Kerry in his arms. "After this, my love," his voice rang out, "after this, it's back to the Philippines with my bride!"

EPILOGUE

Peter and Kerry were married in a garden ceremony because "that's where the first wedding took place."

The Camerons returned to the Philippines after World War II and served the Lord together for 20 years under another mission. This time their ministry was at a Bible college in Manila.

The switch from tribal work in southern Mindanao to teaching in Manila was not easy for Kerry. But she soon discovered that training nationals for Christian service was not turning back from her original vision, but simply plowing in another field. It was especially exciting for Kerry when the first Bilaan enrolled at the school.

It was while the Camerons were in Manila that the good news came that Kerry's father, George McCormick, had recieved Christ as his Savior. Thus one of Kerry's deepest desires was fulfilled.

In consideration of their long and fruitful ministry overseas and in North America, both Kerry and her husband were awarded honorary doctoral degrees.

For additional copies of
The Promise and the Plow
contact your local Christian
bookstore or call
Christian Publications, toll-free,
1-800-233-4443.